# Mahakappina

## The King of Kuluta and the Kinnaras of Himalaya

# Mahakappina

## The King of Kuluta and the Kinnaras of Himalaya

**Tobdan**

**Kaveri Books**
New Delhi - 110002

**Mahakappina: The King of Kuluta and the Kinnaras of Himalaya**
by Tobdan



First Published in 2023
ISBN: 978-93-86463-24-1



Published by

**Kaveri Books**
4832/24, Ansari Road, Darya Ganj
New Delhi - 110 002 (India)
Tel.: 011-47072321
E-mail: kaveribooks@gmail.com
web: www.kaveribooks.com

Typeset by: Aarati Computers, New Delhi

PRINTED IN INDIA

# Preface

Himalaya is vast and varied, possessing high snowy mountains, long river valleys and slopy lands. It has a long history of human settlements. They lived in small groups, each having its own culture, social system, customs, language, etc. They lived much under natural conditions. Due to geographical reasons interaction among them had been difficult and was limited. Their social achievements and religious faiths developed not much beyond the level of their necessities. Under the conditions they could leave very little descriptions about themselves for use by their future generations and others.

Then they came into contact with the people from the larger and advanced societies. They made some notes about these primitive people, as they observed – their appearance, behaviour, etc. Their accounts remained generally short. They were considered as wild, living in the mountains, caves and forests. Sometimes the two had exchange of things. They brought invaluable articles from their inaccessible habitats. Some of their characters were adopted fancifully in the art and literature. They were skilled in jungle games. Therefor they were employed as skilled and trained armies of the rajas and they fought many battles, on both sides, of history and in the Mahabharata.

Mahakappina was a great Teacher. In Pali literature he is a highly respected thera. He was king of the border country named Kukkuta. He was born before the Buddha. This is a way to give the king more honour and place him more close to the Buddha. Evidently Mahakappina's contribution to the Doctrine might have been great.

Then there came traders from Savatthi where there also dwelled the Buddha. On asking about their religion, etc., they told the king that, 'Sire, in our country the Treasure of a Buddha has arisen.' Mahakappina, his men and the traders, all went to the banks of river Chandrabhaga. The Buddha, knowing the fact, came to the banks of Chandrabhaga and ordained Mahakappina. Then they all worked on the banks of Chandrabhaga and in Kuluta. There are remains of Indian Buddhism found in Lahul.

In the Pali literature there are references stating that there lived theras and theris, who call themselves as Kinnara, on the banks of river Chandrabhaga, which stands for Lahul. Evidently there lived Kinnaras on the banks of Chandrabhaga. Rahul Sankrityayan writes that the Kinnaras lived on the western part of the Himalaya and the Kiratas on the eastern.

It is observed that some names given to some ancient people of the Himalayas at a time at one place got changed in the course of long history by another name. It is well known among the scholars that the nomenclature Kimpurusha given to a kind of people was later on replaced by another term Kinnara. Such points may come in the study of the ancient people of the Himalaya.

I am thankful to Prem Lal Yotarpa, Krishan Chandra Mahadevia, C. Dorje, Thilley Shashni, Animesh Prakash, Ram Lal Sharma, Raj Rawal, Internet Archive, and Sh. Rakesh Goel of Kaveri Books.

**Tobdan**

Kullu, April, 2023

# Contents

*Preface* v

*List of Plates* ix

1. Mahakappina Thera: The King of Kuluta 1
2. Kinnaras in Pali Literature: Living on the Banks of River Chandrabhaga 24
3. Kinnaras in History and Art 45
4. Kinnaras: The Different Names and the Historical People 50
5. Kinnara Malana: The Kinnaras of Himalaya 55
6. Kiratas: The Inhabitants of the Eastern Part of the Himalaoya 66
7. The Kiras of Kashmir 79
8. Hiuen Tsiang's *Mo-lo-so* and Other Countries Lying Beyond Kuluta 102
9. Tibetan Pilgrims Going to Jalandhara and Uddiyana: Their Route in Himachal Pradesh 108
10. Approaches to Pangi: A Historical Review 127
11. Lahul: Its Different Names 135
12. Lahul: A Historical Sketch 144
13. A Bird's Eye View of the Geography of the Himalaya 150

*Bibliography* 152

*Index* 161

*Plates* 165

# List of Plates

Cover Photo: Upper portion of the central figure of the Bodhisattva, rock carving at Gundhla.

1. Chhokhor, Tara, of metal.
2. Chhokhor, Bodhisattva image containing inscription in Sharda on the back.
3. Sharda inscription on the back of the image as at 2 above, letters in reverse form.
4. Imprint of the Inscription.
5. Tinan rock carving, three Bodhisattvas.
6. Detail, head of the middle figure of the Tinan rock carving.
7. Boddhisattva on the right of the viewer, Tinan rock carving.
8. gZungs, dhāraṇī, sacred pot, found at the moment of dismantling of the old house built in local style attached to the presently standing castle of Gundhla Thakurs. It was placed in the ground at the time of laying foundation of the house. The earthen pot is painted outside with eight auspicious signs. Inside it was filled with the grains of Ne i.e. huskless barley, moong pulse, etc. There were some precious materials like pieces of gold, pearls, a few other precious stones, etc. There was also a long paper, as seen in the photo, written with a sacred formula. It will appear in a later work. No date was available.
9. Ko-ra, Gyamchhod, 100 lamps. It contains 108 hollows for burning lamps, used earlier. There are other such slabs lying dumped.
10. Kora, Tho, stone cairns on roadside while going downwards from Ko-ra to Gundhla.
11. Kora – Four chhortens, stupa.
12. Gandhala, Drolma Chhudong, Tara, rock carving, photo Wangchuk.
13. Gandhala, Bodhisattva marble head, photo Snellgrove.
14. Gandhala, Lotah, metal vase, incised with designs, photo Birdwood.

15. Srangbar (Khangsar), rock containing the carving.
16. Srangbar, front, Bodhisattva.
17. Srangbar, rock carving, front, smaller figure, left of the viewer.
18. Srangbar, rock carving, Bodhisattva on the backside of the same rock.
19. Khangsar, Khangsar Khar, the Khangsar castle. The attachments in the front of the main castle which might be later additions have now been demolished, c. 1980.
20. Khangsar, Chhukutsi gonpa, Khyung, garuḷa, Eagle, of mixed metal.
21. Kolong, Sangs-rgyas lo-brgyad, Buddha of eight years, Child Buddha, rock carving on granite.
22. Karing, Manye stage or platform, two pillar bases of a probable palatial structure.
23. Karing, manye, detail pillar base-i.
24. Karing, manye, detail pillar base-ii.
25. Karing, mendicant Buddha, tsha- or tshham-par, stamp.
26. Kardang, rock carving, three Bodhisattvas, photo anonymous.
27. Kyelang, Lower Kyelang. Locally called as Dusku (rdo-sku = stone image). There are three images. This is the middle one, the largest one. The images lay on the roadside. The one before whose house it lies is named as Dusku.
28. Zholing 1. Buddha, photo anonymous.
29. Zholing 2. Bodhisattva, photo anonymous.
30. Gushal, two images on stone, unidentified.
31. Triloknath, Chhatra, canopy, gold, over the main statue of Avalokitesvara. In the centre is Buddha sitting encircled by eight Buddhas sitting in the same position.
32. The inner room of the temple of Gepang at Srasrin, Sissu.
33. Khangsar, women weeding and hoeing crop of Rutha, costus, using traditional implement, a small hoe, called surmo.
34. Malana, Jamlung – Jambhala – god of wealth, Jamlu. Refer G.M. Young, 2011 and Chandersain Thakur, Bhrigutung, 2012, Kullu. Photo Tej Ram Negi.

35. Malana, Jaṇāga, platform, the seat of the judges, where they deliberate and deliver judgements, in economic use in other times.

36. Malana, Pīḷhe – the secret vessel – which is brought out only on the day of main Phagli, photo Thara Karadu.

37. Malana, Men converging to the central point of performance of the principal rites on the occasion of the main Phagli, c. February.

38. Malana, women ritually dressed, in a dance pose, in the second Phagli held one month after the main Pahagli, in c. March. They are carrying in their bossom parched saryārā (amaranth) grains which is later on distributed among the participants in the mela, and is eaten, photo anomymous.

39. Malana, Gepang, the body (a long pole) prepared by the men of Malana, being dressed by men of Gepang from Lahul.

40. Malana men, dressed traditionally, main Phagli held in c. Fehruary.

41. Malana men, playing a popular local game famous as pāz.

42. Guge, Chuthak, Burial mask, gold, photo Ritro.

43. Guge, detail of the crown of Chhuthak burial mask, photo Ritro.

44. New Delhi, Yaksha, photo Chattopadhyaya.

45. New Delhi, Yakshee, photo Chattopadhyaya.

# 1

## Mahakappina Thera: The King of Kuluta

Theragatha is an important ancient Pali work which contains life sketches of 264 theras with the contributions from each one of them in verse form. Mahakappina (Mahākappina) is one among them. Mahakappina was king of Kukkuta (Kukkuṭa) or Kukkutavati (Kukkuṭavatī) which was a border country. This country has not yet been identified. However, so far it is being presumed to lie in the north-west India. Mahakappina is a highly praised Thera in the Pali literature. He is given the honour that in the matter of age he is placed at a higher position than the Buddha, stating that he was, "Reborn before our Master's birth." He was a greatly respected Teacher. "He was one of the most eminent disciples of the Buddha, considered foremost among those who taught the monks." He visited the banks of the river Chandrabhaga in order to have view of appearance of the Buddha. Among all the theras given in the Theragatha he is the only one doing so. Buddha perceived that Mahakappina having renounced his kingdom is now coming with his followings to meet him at the banks of the river Chandrabhaga. The Buddha too came from Savatthi through the air and gave his appearance to the king. The king was then ordained by the Buddha.

i. Below we give the description as given about Mahakappina in the Theragatha. "Reborn before our Master's birth in the border country at a town named Kukkuta (Cock), in a raja's family, he was named Kappina. At his father's death he succeeded, as raja, Kappina the Great. He, to extend his knowledge, would send men of a morning out of the four gates to the cross-roads, bidding them arrest passing scholars and tell him. Now by that time our Master had come into the world, and was dwelling at Savatthi. And traders of that town brought goods to Kukkuta and disposed of them. Then saying, 'Let us see the king,' they took gifts and announced themselves. The king accepted their gifts, saluting them, and asked whence they came, and what their country and king were like, and what sort of religion (dhamma) was theirs? 'Sire,' they replied to the last question, 'we are not able to tell you with unwashen mouths.' The king sent for a gold ewer of water, and they, with cleansed mouths and hands at salute, said: 'Sire, in our country the Treasure of a Buddha has arisen.' At the one word 'Buddha,' rapture suffused the king's whole body. "Buddha," say you, friends?' And he made them tell him thrice that infinite word, giving them 100,000 pieces. They told him also of the Treasure of the Norm and of the Order, and he trebled his gift, and forthwith renounced the world, his ministers doing likewise. Now they set forth [to find the Exalted One] and came to the Ganges. There they made a determination by the power of truth, saying: 'If [there be] a Master, a Buddha Supreme, let not even a hoof of these horses be wetted!' Then they crossed on the surface of the full river, and so crossed yet another river, coming thirdly to the great river, Candabhaga, which they crossed in like manner.

'The Master, too, who on that day had risen at dawn, and, filled with great compassion, surveyed the world, discerning that 'to-day Kappina the Great has renounced his kingdom, and comes with a great following to enter the Order; 'tis fit I go far to meet him,' first went with a company of bhikkhus to Savatthi for alms, then went himself through the air to the banks of the Candabhaga, and sat down cross-legged under a great banyan facing the landing-stage of the ford, sending forth the Buddha-rays. Kappina and his men saw the rays darting to and fro, and said: 'We are come on account of the Master, and lo! here He is!' And they drew near, prostrating themselves. Then the Master taught them the Norm, so that they were all established in arahantship, and asked to become recluses. The Master said, 'Come, bhikkhus!' and this was their sanction and their ordination. Then he took them back with him through the air to the Jetavana.

'One day the Exalted One asked whether Kappina taught the Norm to the bhikkhus? They said that he lived in actively, enjoying his happiness. Kappina, when sent for, admitted this was true, and was told: 'Brahmin! do not do so; from to-day teach the Norm to them that have arrived.' Kappina assented, worshipping, and by his very first discourse established a thousand recluses in arahantship.

'Wherefore the Master assigned him the foremost rank among those who taught the Sisters. Now one day the Thera taught the Sisters as follows:

Can ye but see that which is coming ere it come,
'And mark such business as will benefit or harm,
Nor foes nor friends, howe'er they seek, will find a rift.
'The man by whom the breathing exercise
With self-control is to perfection brought,
Practised with method as the Buddha taught,
He casts a radiant sheen about the world,
As doth the moon emerging free from cloud.
Lo! now the mind of me is white indeed,
Expanded beyond measure, practised well,
Its nature understood, and strenuous;
Shedding a radiance on every side.
The wise man is alive and he alone,
Although his wealth be utterly destroyed;
And if the man of wealth do wisdom lack,
For all his wealth he doth not truly live.
Wisdom is arbiter of what is heard.
Wisdom doth nourish honourable fame.
With wisdom in his company a man
Even in pain and sorrow findeth joys.
Here is a fact that's not of yesterday;

This not abnormal nor anomalous:

'Where ye are being born, ye also die.'
What have we there save what is natural?
For after being born we do but lead
A life that is a dying hour by hour.
Whoe'er are born in that same life they die—
Such is the nature of all living things.
That brings no good to the dead which is good for the living.
Mourning the dead is no honour nor purification,
Nor is it praised by the wise, by recluses and brahmins.

Mourning vexes the eye and the body, wasteth
Comeliness, strength [of body and mind] and intelligence.
If he be blithesome, all the four quarters become
Cordial well-wishers, e'en if his lot be not happy.
Wherefore let laymen desire to receive in their family
None but them that are wise and discreet and much learned.
They by the power of their wisdom accomplish their business,
E'en as a boat doth effect a crossing o'er the full river,"
(Davids, 1913:No. 235: 254-257).

ii. Below we give the description about Mahakappina as given by Malalasekera in his dictionary. The description contains some new and important facts about the great thera.

"**Mahakappina Thera:** One of the most eminent disciples of the Buddha, considered foremost among those who taught the monks. He was older than the Buddha, and was born in a frontier kingdom three hundred yojanas in extant in the city of Kukkutavati. On the death of his father he became raja under the name of Mahakappina. His chief wife was Anoja (Anojā) from Sagla in the Madda kingdom. She had been his companion in good works in past births. Every morning Mahakappina would send men out of the four gates of the city to stop any scholarly or learned men who might happen to pass along the road and then return and tell him of them. He owned five horses Vāla, Pupha, Vālavāhan, Puphavāhana and Supatta. Supatta he alone rode. The others were used by his messengers.

'One day after the Buddha's appearance in the world traders came from Savatthi to Kukkutavati and, after disposing their goods, went to see Mahakappina. He received them and asked them about their country and the teachings which they followed. 'Sire,' they replied, 'we cannot tell you without' 'washed mouths.' A golden jug of water was brought and with cleansed mouths and clasped hands they told the king of the appearance of the Buddha. At the word 'Buddha' Kappina's body was suffused with rapture. He made them utter the word three times, giving them a hundred thousand pieces. The men told him also of the Dhamma and the Sangha and he trebled his gifts and forthwith renounced the world followed by his ministers. They set forth to find Buddha and reached the bank of a river which they crossed by an 'Act of Truth,' saying, if this teacher be a

Sammasambuddha, let not even a hoof of these horses be wetted.' In this manner they crossed three rivers. The Aravacchā, the Nīlavāhana and the Candabhāgā. The Buddha perceived them with the divine eye and after he had eaten at Savatthi, went through the air to the banks of Candabhaga and sat down under the great banyan tree facing the landing stage of the river sending forth Buddha rays. Kappina and his men saw him and prostrated themselves. The Buddha taught them the Doctrine and they became arahants and joined the order. The formula 'Ehi Bhikkhu' being their sanction and their ordination.

'Anoja (Anojā) and the wives of the ministers hearing that their husbands had renounced the world and had gone to see Buddha determined to do likewise. They crossed the river in the same way as Kappina and his retinue, and approached the Buddha as he sat under the banyan tree. On the banks of Candabhaga the Buddha made the husbands and wives invisible to each other and preached to the latter. Later they became sotapannas and were ordained by Uppalavanna. The Buddha taking the monks to Jetavana. Mahakappina spent his days in the ecstasy of jhan and also so full of happiness was he that he constantly repeated, 'aho sukham, aho sukham.' Which made suspect that he was longing for the pleasure of kingdom which he had left behind until the Buddha dispelled their doubts.

'One day the Buddha discovered that Kappina lived inactively, enjoying his happiness and he never taught anybody. He sent for him and asked him to teach the Doctrine to his associates. This Kappina did, and at the end of a single sermon thousand listening recluses became arahants, hence the title conferred on him. In the time of Padumuttra Buddha Kappina had registered a vow to become chief among admonishers of monks, having seen a similar honour conferred on a disciple of the Buddha. He was at that time an assessor of Hamsavati, and having invited the Buddha and his monks entertained them with great honour. In another birth he was Kollyan, and waited upon five hundred Pacceka Buddhas and gave them robes. In the time of Kassapa Buddha, he was a leader of a guild of one thousand men and built a great parivena containing one thousand rooms.

'It is said that Kassapa Buddha was preaching and that all the householders of Benaras, with their families, went to hear him. Scarcely had they entered the monastery when there was a heavy downpour of rain. Those who had friends among the novices and monks found shelter in their cells, the others were unprotected. The senior householder suggested that they should build a monastery so that all might be sheltered in future, the others agreeing, he himself gave one thousand each of the other men five hundred, and each woman two hundred and fifty. The monastery had one thousand pinnacles and when money ran short, each gave half as much again. At the dedication ceremony the festival lasted for seven days. The seniormost householder's wife, Anoja, offered the Buddha a casket of anoja-flowers worth one thousand and made a wish that in future births her body should be of the colour of the anoja-flowers.

'Although Kappina was famed as a teacher of monks, Theragatha, curiously enough, contains verses in which he admonishes the nuns.

'It has been remarked that the verses attributed to him are for most part, more gnomic sayings of popular philosophy than genuine Dhamma, and they would have benefitted an early Greek Pagan– Mrs. Rhys David's, interesting theory that Kapina was Assaji's teacher.

'Mahakappina was quite often in the company of Sariputta, and it is said that once seeing the profound homage the gods prayed to his colleague, he smiled by way of congratulation.

'Kappina is described by the Buddha as pale, thin and having a prominent nose. He possessed great iddhi power and had attained every sampatti which could be attained," (Malalasekera, 1938-II: 473-475). The following are two Suttas said in praise of Kappina the Great as given by Malalasekera.

1. '**Kappina Sutta**: Mahakappina visits the Buddha who seeing him from afar tells monks that Mahakappina is highly gifted and of wonderous powers, a gifted preacher and radiant one of those who had gained the object of renunciation. The Buddha proceeded to say how one clothed in wisdom and virtue, is best among beings, and how the Noble One is best of shining objects in that he shines always. The verses of this sutta are also quoted elsewhere.
2. '**Kappina Sutta**: The Buddha sees Mahakappina sitting cross legged with body erect and mindful. He pointed him out to the monks telling them that he can sit like this without shaking or wavering of his body because he has developed concentration on breathing," (Malalasekera, 1937-I:524-25). These are the

words uttered by the Buddha in appreciation of the great thera, Mahakappina.

## Mahakappina Thera: The King of Kukkuta

Theragatha provides that Mahakappina was raja of a border country named Kukkuta. The raja loved scholarship. Now by that time our Master had come into this world and was dwelling at Savatthi. Then traders of that town brought goods to Kukkuta and then they came to see the king.

On asking about their religion, etc., they told the king that, 'Sire, in our country the Treasure of a Buddha has arisen.' They told him also of the Treasure of the Norm and of the Order. The king was impressed. He forthwith renounced the world, his ministers doing likewise. Then they set forth to find the Exalted One coming to the great river Chandrabhaga.

This kind of a great task of influencing a king to get alienated from the worldly affairs and renounce his kingdom cannot be said to be part of the norms of common trading profession. Then the traders had come from Savatthi where there also resided the Buddha. There is named nothing special brought from Savatthi for trading. There is no talk on any matter related to trade even though the traders had come from far off place.

## Majjhima in Kukkuta

It is known that after the conclusion of the Third Buddhist Council, c. 250 B.C.E., under the aegis of emperor Asoka, the farsighted Mogalliputta Tissa, looking at the weakening of the faith in the future in the border countries, advised the theras to go taking with them four other companions each, for the propagation of the faith, taking compassion upon the subjects there. Dipavansa c. C.E. 4-5th century, provides that, in order to generate faith towards the religion among the men there, Majjhima was sent with four other theras: Kassapagotta, Durāsado, Sahadevo, and Mulakadevo, for preaching among the Yaksha people (gaṇa) in the Himavanta, Himalaya. The later work Mahavansa, of about a century later, notes that, Majjhima was sent with other four companions to Himalaya country. It further records that, "The wise Majjhima preached in the Himalaya region, whither he had gone with four theras, the Dhammacakkappavatanasuttanta. Eighty kotis of living beings attained to the reward of the path of salvation. The five theras separately converted five kingdoms, from each of them a hundred thousand received the pabbaja, believing in the doctrine of Sammasambuddha." It gives that five countries in the Himalaya were visited by the missionaries and their subjects were inspired. But we don't find name of any country or people in the work.

These traders from Savatthi were actually the team of the learned theras, the missionaries headed by Majjhima who had been sent from the court of the emperor Asoka for preaching the Faith to the people in the Himalayas. They came to meet Mahakappina in his kingdom Kukkuta, at his capital Kukkuta. They gave discourse on the Dhamma to the king – and his men – who was fully impressed and then entered the path of the Faith. His men followed him. The traders had no talk on trade with the king. Then they all went to the banks of Chandrabhaga. Thus the kingdom of Kukkuta was converted by the missionaries to the Faith. Kukkuta was one of the kingdoms converted by the missionaries sent to the Himalayas.

The Master too discerning that 'to-day Kappina the Great has renounced his kingdom, and comes with a great following to enter the Order, went himself through the air to the banks of the Chandrabhaga, and sat down cross-legged under a great banyan. Kappina and his men saw the Buddha-rays and they drew near, prostrating themselves. Then the Master taught them the Norm, so that they were all established in arahantship, and asked to become recluses.

The literary work Theragatha appears to record to relate complete chain of events of the real history. The proceedings of the story appear to indicate the sequences of events of the same occasion, when the team of the missionaries, messengers of Asokaraja, first might have met the king Mahakappina at Kukkuta. The king, impressed after long discourses given by the team of the learned Theras headed by Majjhima, might have decided to renounce his kingdom and come to the refuge of the Triple Jewels, as did many other kings.

The story of Theragatha that the king of Kukkuta, Mahakappina, was in search of scholars hints at the arrival of the scholar missionaries. They came from Savatthi where there lived the Buddha who was born sometime after Mahakappina. The traders were the missionaries.

## Kukkuta and Kuluta

It is observed that apparently Kukkuta, the name of the capital town of the kingdom of Mahakappina, and also name of the state, matches in form fully with the name Kuluta. Kuluta was name of the ancient state having its capital also named as Kuluta which is presently known as district Kullu in the state of Himachal Pradesh. It is possible that the name Kuluta might have been adapted to Kukkuta to suit the Pali literary form. It is said that Mahakappina, the name of the king of the state, is a monastic name, or may be the name of the ordination. Kukkuta is said to be a border country. Kuluta too is border state and it has been so. With the name of the state and its capital its geography also matches with that given in the story. Kukkuta thus stands for Kuluta.

According to the two sources of Theragatha and Malalasekera, as above, Mahakappina, the king, was born in the capital city of Kukkuta or as Malalasekera writes, in Kukkutavati. Malalasekera in his dictionary explains that in some accounts it is given as Kukkutavati and not Kukkuta. Thus in his view, as he explains taking both the terms, Kukkutavatī was the name of the capital and the name of the state was Kukkuta. Kukkuta is the base of the term Kukkutavati and there is little difference between the two.

Our principal source is Theragatha and the place of the work in Pali literature is well known. In the Theragatha there is only one name Kukkuta which Mrs. Rhys Davids, while translating the work, takes it as the capital town. The same term is found used for state.

We find the term Kukkutavati in the translation of the text of Dhammapala's Atthakatha on Theragatha by Mahinda, given in the next chapter. However, in the original Pali of the Atthakatha edited by Nathamala (1976), as referred to below, Mahakappina was king living in the city of Kukkuta. It writes '*Kukkuta nagara*', 'Kukkuta city.' The name Kukkutavati is not found in the work. It may be elsewhere. Thus Kukkuta is the true name of the capital city and the state.

Thus we see that the ancient sources give the same name both for the capital as well as the state as Kukkuta. Similar is the case with the name Kuluta or Kullu. We read only one name as Kuluta or Kullu in its history, throughout, since ancient to the modern, by one name, both for its capital and the state. Therefor Kukkuta stands for Kuluta. We see further that all other facts in the story and the history match with each other perfectly without slight contradiction.

Malalasekera gives the dimension of the kingdom of Kukkuta or Kuluta as 300 yojanas or 2,700 miles. Hiuen Tsiang gives the dimension of the kingdom of Kuluta as 3,000 li, c. 1,000 miles in circuit. The Kangra district Gazetteer 1897 (part-II:2) gives the dimension of Kullu sub-division at 1934 square miles. The difference in the dimension between that of the ancient and the present Kuluta appears to be slightly wider. It may be, as scholars generally presume, that Kuluta in ancient times might have been larger in area than that we know the state in its history during its medieval and modern period.

Here we may consider a point. Mrs. Rhys Davids writes that, "If for Ganges we substitute Sindhu (the Indus), then Kappina, coming from the extreme north-west, would have the Indus and the Vitasta (Jelum) for his first and second rivers," (Davids,1913: 255, Note-1). The author locates Kukkuta in the 'extreme norh-west.' Since then other scholars have been presuming that this region Kukkuta lay in the north-west India. In fact we have no fact or evidence, or even a hint, to locate Kukkuta anywhere in the north-west. Here on our identification of Kukkuta with Kuluta in the north-east we find that all the related facts, which are in series, automatically get connected.

Cunningham discovered a silver coin from near Kangra, having Buddhist symbols on both sides of it, on which Cunningham read the name of the raja as Vira Yasas of Koluta. He dates it to 100 B.C.E. and classes it among the coins of the Odumbaras, (Cunningham, 1891: 70). But in his account, Cunningham does not include the Koluta or Kulutas among the people named Odumbara. Scholars, however, generally take it for Kuluta.

Kuluta is identified with Kullu. In the seventh century C.E. Kullu was named as Kuluta. Hiuen Tsiang in his diary during his visit to Kuluta in c. C.E. 645 writes the name of the state as Kuluta. He has no other name for its capital. Cunningham writes that, "The kingdom of Kiu-lu-to placed by Hwen Tshang at 700 li or 117 mile, to the north-east of Jalandhar which corresponds exactly with the position of the district of Kullu in the upper valley of Byas river," (Cunninghm, 1924:162-163).

Another indication in the story which matches with the historical fact is that the trader guests were served water by the king from a "Golden Ewer." Gold here indicates to something valuable. The "Golden Ewer" indicates to the intricately carved highly valuable, the ancient, "Lotah" or vase discovered from Gandhala which has been dated as 1st century B.C.E. Gandhala is the place where the king and the missionaries worked extensively.

## Mahakappina: The King of Kuluta

Kappina was born in the kingdom of Kuluta, a frontier country. On the death of his father he became raja under the name of Mahakappina. He belonged to the kshatriya class. His chief wife was named Anojā. She belonged to Sagala, Madda kingdom, in the north-west India. The raja was eager for learning. He was older in birth than the Buddha.

One day a party of traders came from Savatthi. The party of the traders actually was the team of missionaries lead by Majjhima which was sent to the Himalayas by the emperor Asoka. The party told the raja about the Buddha and his Doctrine. Majjhima gave discourses on the Doctrine, particularly on Dhammacakkappavatana. Mahakappina was then impressed from the sermons of Majjhima and renounced the kingdom and entered the refuge of the Triple Jewels.

Then the king Mahakappina with his retinue and the team of Majjhima went crossing the river Beas, across the Rohtang pass. At Khoksar they crossed the Chandra, and then reached at the banks of the river Chandrabhaga, the third river. There on the banks of the river Chandrabhaga the king Mahakappina had vision of appearance of the Great Being. The Buddha had come there himself from Savatthi through the air to give appearance to Mahakappina. Mahakappina was ordained by the Buddha on the banks of river Chandrabhaga.

Mahakappina is highly praised in the Pali literature and is given a very high place among the great Teachers of the Order. Mahakappina was a great Teacher. "By his very first discourse established a thousand recluses in arahantship. Wherefore the Master assigned him the foremost rank among those who taught the Sisters." He was, "One of the most eminent disciples of the Buddha, considered foremost among those who taught the monks." The thera is said to have been born earlier than the Buddha, therefore in age he is senior to the Buddha. The Buddha himself comes to give him appearance on the banks of the river Chandrabhaga. Mahakappina is ordained by the Buddha himself there. There are words for Mahakappina in praise of him from the Buddha himself that, "Mahakappina is highly gifted and of wonderous powers, a gifted preacher and had gained the objective of the renunciation," "Clothed in wisdom and virtue," and more.

Two salient features of Mahakappina are specially emphasised and highlighted. Firstly that he was elder in age from that of the Buddha.

Secondly it is given specially through the mouth of the Buddha himself that Mahakappin is in possession of 'prominent nose'.

This is, infact noted, in the quotation of Malalasekera above about the physiognomy of the king Mahakappina, that also through the mouth of the Buddha, that the king possesses 'prominent nose.' This perhaps indicates to make it clear that 'Mahakappina is not Kinnara.' This is because in the later or other Pali works it is given that the inhabitants of the 'banks of Chandrabhaga' are addressed as Kinnara. Mahakappina went to the 'banks of Chandrabhaga' and worked there among the Kinnaras.

However, we see explained no special contribution made on behalf of the thera towards the Dhamma. But there must have been some contribution notable and extraordinary from his part due to which the thera was accorded so high regard in the literature. Mahakappina was a great historical thera. The notable works done by the missionaries might have been due to him. He was king of one of the countries converted by the party of the Missionaries sent to the Himalaya. He became a great benefactor in the founding and propagation of the Dhamma in the Himalaya. Mahakappina helped the team of the missionaries greatly for long time in accomplishing their works. He aided in the founding of the Dhamma in Kuluta and in the valley of Chandrabhaga. Kuluta was one of the five countries in the Himalaya where the missionaries spread the Doctrine.

The team of Majjhima was benefitted from the presence of the king Mahakappina greatly. They appear to have drawn a big and long term plan for the propagation of the Dhamma in the valley of Chandrabhaga and Kuluta, and other related works to be done extending to long period in the future. These might have included the broad survey of the territory of the banks of river Chandrabhaga, naming the area, the rivers and other natural landmarks. They might have founded religious establishments like viharas, creating followers, teaching the populace and training the teachers, etc.

It is notable that Lahul, which is referred throughout as 'banks of Chandrabhaga' then was an established settlement. It was a settlement of the people large enough among whom propagation of a religion could be made and they could be asked to adopt Buddhism. The missionaries were attracted to the place on two accounts. Firstly its natural features were unique, unavailable elsewhere. Secondly it was inhabited by a different kind of people, the Kinnaras.

**Naming the Rivers:** There is no doubt that the river Chandrabhaga also received its name at the same moment and from the same scholar missionaries.

Lahul lies between the mid-Himalaya or the Pir Panjal range and the Bara-lacha or the Western Himalayan range. Its geographical area constitutes the valleys of the two rivers of Chandra and Bhaga, which are the two heads of Chandrabhaga, some part of the valley of the combined Chandrabhaga and the area encircled by the two rivers. The two rivers Chandra and Bhaga originate on either side of the Baralacha pass and then meet at some distance after covering long courses. There are two corresponding lakes named Chandratal and Surajtal. The mountain tip lying at the confluence between Chandra and Bhaga was named as Chanda or Chandra, which name is now lost.

The missionaries surveyed the geography of the whole region: thoroughly, particularly the courses of the two remarkable rivers and the great mass of land encircled by the two. This great laborious work was done by the missionaries sent in the time of Asoka's reign to the Himalaya which was headed by Majjhima, (Tobdan, 2021a: 13). They propagated the Dhamma among the inhabitants who were recognised as Kinnara. They also trained the group of the Malana villagers, who might have been there somewhere around the area, in the complex form of village administration which they have kept live in practice, guarded ever at the new settlement. It would be interesting to compare it with the system existing in the Buddhist period. We gather some data on the geographical marks of Lahul, as surveyed by the missionaries, from the various modern scholars.

### The Courses of the two rivers and the Great Triangle or the Central Lahul

Gandhala is the central point of the geography of Lahul and it has also historically been the centre of religious and cultural activities. Gandhala is situated on the tip of the nose of the range ending at the confluence between Chandra and Bhaga. The range starts from Baralacha pass from where also originate the two rivers. This great land mass encircled by the two rivers is triangular in shape. In the Gazetteer of 1897 it is named as 'the Great Triangle' and McArthur, a surveyer and a mountaineer, names it as the 'Central Lahul'. This chunk of the land mass played pivotal role in the naming of the river Chandrabhaga. This name is formed of joining the names of the two rivers which encircle the great mass of land and are also the headwaters of the river Chandrabhaga. The admirable shape of this mass of land lends names to the two rivers and subsequently to the main river Chandrabhaga.

**Central Lahul**: McArthur writes that, "The Central Lahul is a rough triangle with the apex in the north at the Bara Lacha pass. The triangle is bounded on two sides by the Chandra and on the third side by Bhaga river. The upper Chandra is uninhabited and almost without vegetation other than some grass and many alpine flowers. In summer many nomadic shepherds drive flocks from one meadow to the next," (McArthur, 1956: 279-295). The team conducted survey of the top of the Central Lahul under the authority of the Survey of India in 1955 in the name of 'Central Lahul Expedition 1955.' The fringes of Central Lahul had been touched by two previous expeditions, one in 1939 and another just before that of the present one. This time the team surveyed the top snowy plain.

Cunningham provides detailed geographical data about the rivers– the two heads of the river and the main river – covering the complete course from its origin to the point of its junction with the Indus. He writes, "Chandra and the Bhaga rise on opposite sides of the Bara Lacha pass, in N. latitude 32" 45' and E. longitude 77"22' at an elevation of 16,500 feet above the sea. The Chandra flows at first to the south for fifty five miles and then sweeps suddenly up to the north west for sixty miles further, to the junction of the Bhaga river at Tandi. The fall to this point is 7,500 feet, or sixty five feet per mile, for the Chandra river, and 125 feet per mile for the Bhaga river, which has a course of only sixty miles to the southwest. At Koksar, twenty five miles above Tandi and 10,000 feet above the sea, the Chandra river averages 200 feet in width, with a mean depth of two and a half feet, and a current of not less than four miles per hour in October when it is fordable with very great difficulty. The discharge at that time is therefore not less than 2000 cubic feet. From Tandi the Chander Bhaga pursues a north westerly course to Kishtwar, a further distance of 115 miles. The whole length to this point is 330 miles, and the fall is 11,500 feet, or 34.8 feet per mile, (Cunningham, 1854: 118). Thus we see that the large triangular block is encircled from three sides by the two rivers of the length of 60 (Bhaga)x55x60 miles. The river has got much weakened since then.

**The Great Triangle**: The Gazetteer of 1897 gives geography of the region stating that, "The great triangle formed by the Candra and Bhaga is filled up by an off shoot from the range to the north; its peaks rise to 21, 20 and 19,000 feet, and its numerous lateral valleys are all filled with glaciers. It is one great ice-bed, broken here and there by lofty heights of impassable rock and snow. To the south of the highest peak, 21,415 feet, stretches a vast glacier, 12 miles in length, which is met by another of even greater dimensions. The most noted peak, though not the highest, is the Gephang Lha, or God Gephan, in whose honour the Lahulis hold feasts and make sacrifices. This is the snowy cone which can be seen from the Kulu valley through a gap in the mid-Himalaya. The most noted glacier in Lahul is that known as the big Shigri at the bend of the Chandra on its south side. It is nearly two miles wide and runs right down to the river; the marks are still to be seen throughout Lahul of the destruction caused many years ago by a portion of the glacier having fallen across the river and dammed up the water until the melting of the ice released the pent-up flood," (Gazetter: 1897-III:2).

Between Khoksar and Tandi there are three passes on this range. The first lies between Darcha and Khoksar, the two villages being situated on the banks of Bhaga and Chandra respectively. It was seldom used by the local people. It is said to be difficult and its name is also not known. Another one named Dāngrā lies between Tinno, on Bhaga, and Sissu in Chandra valley. It was used but perhaps not customised. The distance is measured in the manner that if ḍakur, yeasted cake of buckwheat, is taken warm in a bag it remains warm till the traveller reached Sissu. It is about a half day's journey.

**Kora or Rangtsa**: The third pass is named as Kora (skor-ra, ko-rā = circumambulation) or Rangtsa (= pass, in Tinani). It is situated between Kardang and Gundhla. This is a sacred circumambulation pilgrimage route. The kora route starts from Kardang and crossing the pass reaches Gundhla. Performance of this pilgrimage was considered very enjoyable and was very popular specially among the young and the women. The other two pilgrimages are to Rebag (Triloknath) and mTsho (Riwalsar). The people go in large groups. Then people come back through Tandi. But earlier they used to return through below the Gandhala monastery to Kardang. On the top of the pass there are some chhortens (mchhod-rten = worship raising), chaityas, unplastered and different in shape from those seen in the valley in Lahul. The main cluster of four chhortens, in a row, is at the top where there is also a small shed for mchod-me (worship-fire), for lighting worship lamps. There are some old discarded stone slabs on which are engraved hollows to function as worship lamps. About half a dozen chhortens are situated raised at some distance from the present site. Along the path down to Gundhla there are raised on the edges of the path a number of *tho,* stone cairns. This kora is done in the summer mostly when the people have a small time of leisure after the hard pressing work of the sowing season is over. The second heavy season comes after the work of harvesting and thrashing is finished. Lahul gets only one crop in a year for which every effort has to be made to make it successful as much as possible and no chance is left to negligence. It is known as the Dril-bu Ri'i sKor-ra, circumbulation of Drilbu Ri. The mountain peak in the centre is named as Drilbu Ri, Bell mountain, Ghanta-parvata. There is also situated the Gandhala monastery somewhat below. There is an image of Dolma, Tara, there carved on a boulder. It is named as Dolma Chhu-dong (water hollow, through which flows water). It is believed that water flows under the rock containing the image. The carved image is situated on a sharp cliff, on the shorter and difficult route where only a few young and accustomed to mountain walking can go. It is an ancient remnant of Indian Buddhism and is a rare kind of work. It depicts an excellent workmanship done on stone.

There is the great glacier of Shigri (Louse-mount; shig = louse; ri = mount) which got burst and it flooded in 1836. The glacier blocked the river Chandra. The great wool market located in the upper Chandra valley where traders from Jangthang, Lahul, Spiti, Kinnaur, Kullu, etc. used to gather annually, was destroyed and then it was established at Dozam, Patseo, in Lahul, and another one in Spiti, (Tobdan, 2021a: 213-237). The party of survey climbed up to the top plain of the Central Lahul through near this glacier.

It is this great mass of land which became symbol and facilitated in naming the rivers, lakes and the mountain of the region. The great mass of land, whose geographical details we studied above, is in scientific language called as 'Great Triangle.' Poetically it is or is like the crescent Moon and practically Chandrabhāga, 'portion of the Moon.' Thus this mass of land is Chandrabhāga, portion of the Moon.

Break up of this term Chandrabhāga lends names to the two rivers encircling it as Chanda or Chandra (= Moon) and Bhāga (= portion, or part). The two after joining at Tubchiling provide name of the main river as Chandrabhāga or Chandrabhāgā which flows long to meet Sindhu. At the point of its junction with the Sindhu it was known to the Greek scholars as Chandrabhaga. Practically we speak and write as Chandrabhāgā instead of Bhāga. In the Pali literature also we find the same form of the term. But this is the only way we can explain it. The two rivers originate at one place on either side of Bara Lacha (pa-ra = cross; la-rtse = pass-top: top of the pass which is like a cross) and join at Tubchiling. Tandi and Gushal, both situated close to the confluence, are situated on the right and left side of Bhāgā and Chandra respectively. It is possible that at the same time name also might have been given to the country although the Pali literature makes it known in history by the name as 'the banks of river Chandrabhaga.' Hiuen Tsiang names it as Lahul.

As regards the cause for the selection of the region by the team of the learned theras, one reason is obvious, the uniqueness of geography of the headwaters of the river Chandrabhaga. The two rivers originating at one place, flowing in two different directions encircling a great mass of land in the shape of the crescent Moon, each having a lake near its origin, and then again meeting at a place at some distance, is absolutely unique. This is the main reason of their attraction to the spot. They surveyed, gave names to important geographical marks, and worked in the area and among the people. They gave a permanent place to the region in history.

Thus the valley became famous as the 'banks of river Chandrabhaga,' a holy place. There also might have started works on creating some structures. Theras and theris started coming from distant places. It became a place of congregation for the theras and theris of distant places. At Gandhala at the height where there used to be the monastery earlier there is a pleasant large flat land. It is possible that the ancient and the earliest monastery might have existed there. The ancient artefacts were also discovered from there or nearby it.

It cannot be said that the thought arose suddenly in the mind of the team, including Mahakappina, to go across the Rohtang pass and explore further. Then a liking arose for the banks of the river Chndrabhaga. This is a deserted wild and has very difficult geography. Then they did not stay in Kuluta, the pleasant and beautiful place, or return from there. Firstly they were a dedicated people in possession of some great objective in their mind. Some knowledge of the geography of the place must have been already with them and they must have had a plan to found a permanent establishment for the regular visit of the pilgrims from the distance places.

They had knowledge about the place since the time of the Buddha, the Chanda-Kinnara jataka.

## History of the river Chandrabhaga

**Asikni and Asita:** The history and geography of the river Chandrabhaga has already been discussed in detail, (Tobdan, 2021: 1-23). Here it is given briefly with a new source strengthening our earlier presentation about its folk name given at its end. The Vedic name of Chandrabhaga at its end where it joins with Indus is given as Asikni. Rigveda gives a list of some prominent rivers as: Ganga, Yamuna, Sarasvati, Shutudri, Parushni, Marudvrdha, Asikni, Vitasta, Arjikiya and Sushoma. It mentions among others name of Asikni also which the scholars identify with Chandrabhaga. Nirukta, called a Vedang, which is stated to be, "the oldest Indian treatise on Etymology, Philology and Semantics,' and treats Vedic terminologies," also gives a similar list with almost the same names including Asikni, (Laksman, 1967- Eng. Tr.: 147).

Nirukta further states that, "The word *sitam* is synonym of white colour, its antithesis is *a-sitam*." It appears to refer to the pre-Vedic names of the two great rivers of Sindhu and Asikni as Sita (sitam) and Asita (a-sitam), as recognised earlier. This confirms our earlier presentation that the two rivers Sindhu and Asikni or Chandrabhaga were formerly named as Sita and Asita.

Nirukta explains Asikni as 'non-bright' or 'non-white.' Monier-Williams and McCrindle translate Asikni as dark-coloured. Thus the pre-Vedic folk names of the two rivers Sindhu and Asikni or Chandrabhaga were Sita and Asita.

Asita merges with the Sita at Mithankot, in Pakistan, and loses its identity permanently. The name Asita was also forgotten in due course. The other name Sita continued in existence in literature, throughout the history alongwith its Vedic name, although without knowledge of its significance. The name Sita sometimes was transformed to some other forms and sometimes was used to indicate some other river.

Thus the river has four names: Asita, Asikni, Chandrabhaga and Chenab, in the sequence of time of receiving the name. Scholars also identify the name Marudvrdha with Chandrabhaga. The first is the folk and the earliest name. Others are all literary names. The first is Vedic and the next is Pali. Of all these the first two were named at the end of the river and the third name was given at its head. The last, a literary name was given at the last in time. Although it purports to have been given at its head but it locates the source of the river in Kishtwar. Thus we understand the importance of the river Chandrabhaga which receives all the Punjab rivers having long and rich history.

## Buddhism in Kuluta

About the situation of Buddhism in Kuluta, Hiuen Tsiang when he visited Kuluta in c. C.E. 645 writes that, "There are about twenty sangharamas and 1000 priests or so. They mostly study the Great Vehicle, a few practice the rules of other schools, nikayas. There are fifteen Deva temples, different sects occupy them without distinction." The scholar traveller also writes that, "In the middle of the country is a stupa built by Asokaraja. Of old the Tathagata came to this country with his followers to preach the law and to save men. This stupa is a memorial of the traces of his presence," (Beal 1884-iv: 177).

As we have learnt above that at the time of visit of the missionaries sent by the emperor Asoka, Mahakappina was the king of Kuluta. Mahakappina adopted Buddhism and worked with the missionaries extensively. He is ranked amongst the highest of the few Teachers of the faith in whole of the Pali literature. He is given place closest to the Buddha. He went with the missionaries to the banks of Chandrabhaga and worked there with them. Similarly he must have worked with the missionaries in his own state. This included the work of founding of the stupa in the state. This immensely great task must have been executed with the efforts and association of the great king and teacher Mahakappina who facilitated the visit of the Asoka the Great to his kingdom of Kuluta. Asoka the Great visited Kuluta and with the assistance of Mahakappina got the stupa erected in the middle of the Kuluta country in memory of the visit of the Great Being to the place as has been stated, as above, by HiuenTsiang. In this connection there is the Chanda-Kinnara jataka which story was enacted on the Chanda-parvata i.e. mount Gandhala across Rohtang pass. The Pali literature has placed these descriptions with the highest regard. On this point we have spoken already, (Tobdan, 2008). Ashokaraja and Mahakappina were historically two great contemporaneous emperor and king.

## Buddhism in Lahul

In Lahul Indian Buddhism, which was introduced by the team headed by Majjhima, remained actively present for long time. At Gandhala there were discovered some artifacts of archaeological importance. At Chhokhor in Sissu there are remains of Indian Buddhism like the metal statue of Tara, the small Boddhisattva icons with Sharda inscription and the monastery of Triloknath, its structure, statues and the inscription. There are several carvings of Bodhisattvas on rocks of the period of Indian Buddhism, on the roadsides at different places in Chandra and Bhaga valleys.

**Gandhala Monastery:** The two pilgrim lamas of the thirteenth-fourteenth century from Tibet Gozangpa and Urgyanpa write the name of the place as Gandhala. In the local Bhoti literature Gandhala is also found written as Gandhola and the mountain peak situated at some distance above is known as Drilbu Ri. This is a later name perhaps related to Drilbu-pa, Ghantā-pāda, one of the 84 siddhas. In sTod it is pronounced as Gandhala. Some scholars trace origin of the name from the Sanskrit word Gandhālaya, house of aroma, from Bodhgaya. At the confluence of the rivers Chandra and Bhaga, in between the two, there is a small plateau called Tubchiling, about twenty meters above the river bed. Earlier there used to be structures for the night stay for the pilgrim lamas and resting place for the pilgrims. Now the monastery has been shifted down to here. Above this about a kilometer above there is the second flat plateau. The monastery of Tibetan tradition exists here, although all the artefacts of the monastery have been brought down. The ancient monastery of Indian Buddhism also might have been situated at the same place. This is a wide about one by one kilometer beautiful place. Gozangpa gives dimension of the place equal to one dpag-tshad i.e. c. 24,000 feet. There is also a gnas-bshad, pilgrimage guidebook in the names of Gandhola and Drilbu Ri.

An engraved lotah, vase, of a mixed metal, was discovered in 1857 by Major Hay, the first Asstt. Commissioner of Kullu Sub-division which comprised Lahul and Spiti also, from Gandhala, Lahul. It was examined by Charles Horne and he dates it C.E. 200-300. He remarks that, "It has evidently been treated with the greatest care; for we do not find upon it any signs of the constant polishing with sand and ashes which the lotahs of the natives undergo when in constant use, and which in a few years wears them quite thin.... In 1857 Major Hay, then in Political Employ in the Kulu country, which comprises the districts of Lahoul and Spiti, in the Himaleh, happening to be near Goondlah, heard that some curious ancient vessels had been found near the junction of the Chandra and Bhaga (Bhagur) rivers not far distant. It would appear that upon the spot had formerly stood a Buddhist monastery, and that owing to a great landslip a vaulted chamber or hollow had been laid bare, in which were found this brass vase, and some dishes of kassa," (Charles Horne, 1871: 367). Charles Horne further writes that the whole of the exterior, with the exception of a part of the neck, is covered with engraving. First there is a young prince in a chariot or car drawn by four horses abreast. The whole is a royal procession scene, certainly prince Siddhartha. Later on the lotah has been re-examined and it is now dated 1st century B.C.E. (Errington & Cribb, 2012:163-164). There also exists an image of Tara locally known as Dolma Chhu-dong, at the circumambulation path at the top of the ridge, carved on a rock exquisitely.

Basham affirming the importance of the find object, has published full picture of the lotah and the carvings on it with the remarks that, "Wholly Indian in style, and dating from pre-Gupta times, is the copper vase from Kulu, on the borders of Kashmir, engraved with a gay procession," (Basham, 1954:374 ).

Snellgrove visited the monastery in 1953. He describes the condition of the establishment. He writes, "In 1953 it presents itself as one of the smallest and certainly the most neglected of the Lahuli monasteries, because being in charge of one solitary monk. There are remains of ancient wood work without, and inside standing amongst images of recent workmanship on the altar is the head of a bodhisattva, which had been dug up in the valley below. Is this a possible example preserved from the time when Kulu was a Buddhist land. It shows a striking rsemblance to some Central Asian models,' (Snellgrove, 1957: 293, Note-39). It was extremely fortunate that Snellgrove photographed the marble head of the bodhisattva and he published it in his book. The artefact was lost soon thereafter to big thieves. The monastery is now satisfied with a crude model of it, received in exchange, enshrined at the most sacred place and keeping it under guard.

Pali literature has extensive references stating that there lived Kinnari and Kinnara theras on the banks of river Chandrabhaga. This certainly refers to the region constituting the headwaters of Chandrabhaga, the present Lahul, particularly the confluence. These are verses written by the Theris and Theras themselves who tell that they lived as Kinnari and Kinnara on the banks of river Chandrabhaga in one of their ancient lives when they were born as Kinnari or Kinnara there. These are now found in the collections like Therigatha, Apadana, etc. Mahakappina, the king of

Kuluta, also visited the banks of Chandrabhaga and there he had the view of the appearance of the Great Being.

The Chanda-Kinnara jataka, one of the most important among all the jatakas, provides that the Great Being, in one of his former life as a Bodhisattva and his beloved Yashodhara, lived in the Himalaya, in the life of fairy, Kinnara and Kinnari. The two were named as Chanda and Candā and lived on the mountain named Chanda-Parvata. The stage of enactment of the story was Chanda Parvata. This has been identified with the mount Gandhala, situated at the confluence of the rivers Chandra and Bhaga, (Tobdan, 2008: 459-464). This is so because there could not be found any mountain with which the name Chanda Parvata could be identified. Here there exist strong hints pointing to the existence of the mountain with the name Chanda as there exist several geographical marks around it with similar names. Here there are the rivers connected with the name as Chandra, Chandrabhaga and the lake named Chandratal connected with the two rivers. Therefore existence of the Chanda mountain in the environment becomes meaningfully relevant. This mountain is historically famous as Gandhala.

The banks of the river Chandrabhaga were also sanctified by the footfalls of the Great Being. HiuenTsiang writes that the great Emperor Asoka raised the stupa at Kuluta in memory of the visit of the place by the Buddha. In this pure and the great act Mahakkapina, the great thera and the king of Kuluta was intimately associated who facilitated the visit of the emperor Asoka and got the stupa raised. The Chanda-Kinnara jatak, one of the most important and the ancient jataka, provides that the Great Being, in one of his former life as a Bodhisattva and his companion Yashodhara, enacted the whole story in the life of Kinnara and Kinnari on the Chanda-parvata which lies on the banks of Chandrabhaga.

**Theragatha: Its Place in Pali Literature:** About the Theragatha, it is given that of the collection of fifteen works in the Khuddaka Nikaya, forming part of Sutta Pitaka, Theragatha and Therigatha are the 8th and 9th and Apadana the 13th work. B.C. Law writes about Theragatha that, "It is a collection of poems, some of which are believed to have been sung by theras during the lifetime of the Buddha, and others shortly after his parinirvana. These poems are conducive to the understanding of the religious theories and feelings prevalent in the Buddhist Order," (B.C.

Law,1933- I: 264-65). Here we learn about its importance and antiquity of the works.

We give our understanding of the works referred to here based on the matters dealt with. We try to give them in a rough chronological order. Chanda-Kinnara Jataka referring to Chanda-parvata is the first related to the area. It does not refer directly to the area but appears indirectly referring to Lahul. Theragatha gives life of one thera who visited the banks of river Chandrabhaga. This Thera Mahakappina was an important historical person. We know the period to which he belonged. He helped the missionaries sent by emperor Asoka to the Himalayas. In the Therigatha there are three theris who in their verses reveal that they were born in one of their former lives as Kinnari and they lived on the banks of river Chandrabhaga. There are other theras and theris described in Dharampal's Atthakatha and the Apadana who lived on the banks of the river Chandrabhaga. These indicate that many theras and theris visited the holy place, the banks of river Chandrabhaga.

Thus Buddhism came and was founded on the banks of the river Chandrabhaga, Lahul, in the time of emperor Asoka, by the missionaries sent by the emperor for preaching the Doctrine among the people of the border countries in the Himalaya. Mahakappina, the king of Kuluta, was fully associated with the process. Lahul lay on the branch path of the International Silk Route leading through Kullu, Lahul, Ladakh, etc. and linking the fertile and productive plains of north and north-west India and the rich silk markets like Kashgar, etc. of Central Asia.

# 2

## Kinnaras in Pali Literature
### Living on the Banks of River Chandrabhaga

In Pali literature there are descriptions about the Kinnaras living in the Himalaya. Some works write that Kinnaris and Kinnaras live on the banks of the river i. e. in the valley of Chandrabhaga. This certainly must be at the head of the river which may be identified with the present Lahul.

Rahul Sankrityayan writing about Kinnaur in his work 'Kinnardeshme', quotes the sentence 'candrabhāgā nadītīre ahosi kinnarī tadā,' – stated to be from Vimanvatthu of Suttapitaka of the second-third century B.C.E., (Rahul, 1948: 291-292). It states that there lived Kinnaris on the banks of Chandrabhaga. Rahul from the phrase 'on the banks of river Chandrabhaga,' means Lahul, situated at the headwaters of the river, as he says that Kinnara language is still spoken there. Upadhyaya quotes the same sentence, from a different source, from Pramatthadipani of Dhammapala, and affirms that there lived Kinnaris on the banks of Chandrabhaga, (Upadhyaya, 1947: 62, Note-5). Apadana completes the expression by giving the complementary sentence: candabhāgā nadī tīre ahosiṃ kinnaro tadā, (Jagdish, 1959-I: 282), 'There live Kinnaras on the banks of river Chandrabhaga.' Thus there lived both Kinnaris and Kinnaras on the banks of river Chandrabhaga. These sentences are parts of the verses written by the learned Theris and Theras, monks, who proclaim that they in the past in the life of Kinnara lived on the banks of river Chandrabhaga. They might have lived there but they were not Kinnara and not the inhabitants of the place. But this avers that the place was inhabited by Kinnaras.

Below we give descriptions about the Kinnaras from the various Pali works.

### A. Kinnaras in the Jatakas

Some Jatakas describe Kinnaras living in the Himalaya and highlight some of their characteristics. Cowell, and also some others, translate the term Kinnara or Kinnari, contained in the texts, as 'fairy.'

i. **Kandina Jataka, no. 13**: The Jataka tells that the Buddha was once born in the former life as a fairy, Kinnara. The Great Being tells, "In those days the love-sick Brother was the mountain stag, his mundane wife was the young doe, and I was myself the fairy who preached the Truth shewing the sin of passion." Here the Buddha takes the form of a Kinnara and preaches the Law.

ii. **Bhallatiya Jatak, no. 504:** There lived Kinnaras on the Gandhamadan mountain beyond the Himalaya.

iii. **Sama Jataka, no. 540:** It is told that the Kinnaras live on the Gandhmadan mountain beyond the Himalaya. They lived in the caves and collected fruits. The Kinnara couple bathed a newborn child of a couple who had come from Benaras for living in the forests to lead the life of an ascetic. They are friendly to the strangers.

iv. **Sarabha-Miga Jataka, no. 483:** The story tells that the Kinnaras, who lived in the Himalayas, is a rare being. Kinnaras have good quality of singing and dancing and they are intelligent. This is a story of a couple of Kinnaras caught by a hunter who then presented them to the king of Benaras. The moral of the story is given as, "They who are moderate of speech, by watching their words have often been freed from the fate of death."

    Kinnaras live in the Himalaya. They are seen rarely and are a rare being. Their foremost quality is that they 'can sing with a honey-voice, they dance delightfully!' We also learn that they, 'have sung a hundred thousand songs.' This indicates that they have their own language which is well advanced. They compose songs in their own language and sing. But they cannot please the others because they cannot convey the meanings of the songs to others.

v. **Chanda-Kinnara Játaka and the Chanda-Parvata Jataka no. 485:** The Great Being, in one of his former life as a Bodhisattva and his beloved Yashodhara, took birth in the Himalayas, in the life of fairy, Kinnara and Kinnari. The two were named as Chanda and Candā and lived on the mountain named Chanda-Parvata. This

Chanda Parvata has been identified with the mount Gandhala situated on the confluence of the rivers Chandra and Bhaga, (Tobdan, 2008: 459-464).

**B. Kinnaras in Other Pali Works**

There are some other Pali works where the descriptions are more extensive and realistic showing the Kinnaras as a living people. Here their presence is much widely spread over the Himalaya and beyond. Specially they are shown living in greater number on the banks of river Chandrabhaga. This area appears to have been inhabited by the people known as Kinnara. The extensive material about the Kinnaras on this aspect is impressive.

These works may be named as Theragatha, Therigatha, two works named Pramathadipani – the commentaries by Dhammapala on Theragatha and Therigatha – and lastly Apadana which consists of two parts: Therapadana and Theriapadana. We get the first glimpse of the subject in Theragatha where, however, there is description of only one Thera who met the Buddha on the banks of the river Chandrabhaga. He was not a Kinnara. Therigatha contains stories of more than one Theri living on the banks of Chandrabhaga. Dhammapala's commentaries are naturally subsequent works. Apadana is said to be the latest canonical work but containing lives of some earlier teachers also. The nature of these works is of Gatha, stories in verse. These verses were written by the Theras and Theris themselves. In them they are relating their previous life stories. The lives described in the works include those of some of the most important persons of the Order and many of them are stated to be historical. Scholars identify some of the Theras and Theris found described in the Therapadana and Theriapadana with those found described in the Theragatha and Therigatha,

I. **Theragatha:** In the Theragatha there is found description of only one Thera, Mahakappina, Kappina the Great, about whom it is told that he met the Buddha on the banks of river Chandrabhaga. We have already read about this Thera.

II. **Paramatthadipani, Dhammapala's Commentary on Theragatha (Atthkatha)**

   a. **Theragatha, Commentary:** In the Commentary on Theragatha by Dhammapala there are four Theras including the one described above who lived on the banks of river

Chandrabhaga, as: 1. Uttiya Thera (Book-1, section-3, No. 10), 2. Sīha Thera (Book-1, section-9. No.-3), 3. Sambhūta Thera (Book-2, section-4, No.-7). 4. Mahākappina Thera (Book-2, section-10, No.-3), (Nathamala, 1976). Of these Siha and Sambhuta are told to have been born in the life of Kinnara and lived on the banks of river Chandrabhaga. The other two visited the banks of river Chandrabhaga.

These are found described in English translation in Theragathapali, a work by Mahinda. We give below some essential facts about these theras from the work.

**b. Theragathapali**

i. **Siha Thera:** Siha Thera was born in the family of a raja in the Malla country and visited the Buddha. The Buddha taught him a discourse suitable to his temperament, and he entered the Order. He lived in the forests in meditation but his thoughts were distracted. The Buddha seeing thus went through the air and spoke to him alone, asking him to persevere. Thus incited he strove hard and attained arhantship. He was once a kinnara on the banks of Chandrabhaga and seeing Atthadassa Buddha journeying through the air, stood still, gazing at him with clasped hands. Then Buddha alighted and sat under a tree where the Kinnara offered him flowers and sandalwood. Siha was three times king under the name of Rohini. He is probably identical with Candanpujaka of Apadana.

ii. **Sambhuta Thera:** Sambhuta Thera belongs to a family of clansman and joined the Order under Anand Thera after the Buddha's death, attaining Arhantship in due course. In the past, during the period when there were no Buddhas in the world, Sambhuta was a kinnara on the banks of the Candrabhaga, and seeing Pacceka Buddha, he worshipped him and offered ajjuna flowers. He is evidently identical with Ajjunpuphiya of Appadana.

iii. **Mahakappina Thera:** Mahakappina Thera was one of the most eminent desciples of the Buddha, foremost among those considered who taught the monks. He was older than the Buddha, and was born in a frontier kingdom, three hundred leagues in extent, Kukkutavati. On the death of his father he became king under the name of Mahakappina.

iv. **Uttiya Thera:** It is recorded that, Uttiya was the son of a brahmin of Sāvatthi. When he came of age, he left the world, seeking "the Deathless," and became a wanderer

III. **Therigatha:** In the Therigatha there are three Theris who say that they were born as Kinnari and they lived on the banks of river Chandrabhaga. These are – 1. Theri Puṇṇā, 2. Another 'Sāmā,' and 3. Dantikā.

Before we give the lives of the Theris, we place below some facts gathered from their life stories:

i. The verses were written by the Theris themselves. They convey that they were born Kinnari from the Kinnari mothers. As such they were Kinnari themselves born at the banks of river Chandrabhaga. About Theri Dantikā it writes, "At that time I was a kinnari on the banks of …." "At a time without a [teaching] Buddha she was born in the womb of a kinnari on the banks of the river Candabhāgā," (William Pruitt, 1998: 70-71).

ii. The Theris lived in the society of Kinnaras. It is said about Theri Dantikā, "One day while playing and walking about with the kinnaras she saw certain Pacceka Buddha seated at the foot of a certain tree as his daytime resting place," (William Pruitt, 1998: 71). Dantika was walking about with the Kinnaras, as she was living in the community of Kinnaras, in the area inhabited by the Kinnaras, on the banks of river Chandrabhaga.

iii. Birth of the Theris in the life of Kinnari was an event of long past. It was their previous life. Dhammapala writes about Theri Citta, "Ninety-four aeons ago she was born in the womb of a kinnari on the banks of …," (William Pruitt, 1998: 48).

iv. The Theris who have lived the life of Kinnari previously, are presently living in the human world like all. About Theri Citta, Dhammapala writes, "In this Buddha era she was born in the home of a wealthy householder in Rajagah," (William Pruitt, 1998: 49). Theri Citta in the present life is born in the home of a householder in Rajgrih. She now remembers her previous birth in the life of Kinnari, born and living on the banks of the river Chandrabhaga.

v. Some of the Theris relate that when they were born in the life of Kinnari it was the period when there was no Teaching of Dhamma on the banks of river Chandrabhaga. About Theri Puñña it is said, "She was reborn of a kinnari on the banks of the river Candabhāgā in a world period without a [teaching] Buddha," (William Pruitt, 1998: 16). From this we may construe that the Kinnara people living on the banks of river Chandrabhaga had not yet received the teachings of the Buddha. The inhabitants were ignorant and they had not yet gone into the refuge of the Dhamma.

vi. But subsequently the light of the Dhamma had appeared on the land of the Kinnaras. The other 'Theri Sāmā' remembers that, "At the time of the Blessed One Vipassi, she was reborn in the womb of a kinnari on the banks of the river Candabhāgā. And she lived there intent on play together with the other kinnaras," (William Pruitt, 1998: 63). Now there is the light of the teachings of the Buddha shining on the Kinnaraland. The inhabitants are blessed with the teachings of the Great Lord.

Below we give accounts in abstract of the descriptions about the Theris from Therigatha:

**i. Punna (Puṇṇā):** The related verse is that of a student named Punna. She, heaping up good of age-enduring efficacy under former Buddhas in this and that state of becoming, was born – when the world was empty of a Saviour Buddha – as a fairy, by the River Candabhaga, (Davids, 1909: 11-12).

**ii. Another Sama ('Sāmā'):** She also, heaping up good like the foregoing, was born, in the time of Vipassi Buddha, as a fairy on the banks of the River Candabhaga, (Davids, 1909: 34-35).

**iii. Dantika (Dantikā):** She, too, having made her resolve under former Buddhas, and in this and that rebirth heaping up good of age-enduring efficacy, was born, when the world was empty of a Buddha, as a fairy by the river Candabhaga, (Davids, 1909: 37-38).

**IV. Paramatthadipani, Dhammapala's Commentary on Therigatha (Atthakatha)**: The work contains descriptions of all the three Theris, as above, and adds the fourth named as Theri Citta. She was born Kinnari and lived on the banks of river Chandrabhaga.

Muller, Editor of the work in the Introduction gives descriptions of some Theris coming under the heading "at the time of Buddha Vipassi." Here, among others, there is description about Theri Sama, whom he describes as 'was born as kinnari on the banks of river Chandrabhaga.' We reproduce the same as under:

**Sāmā:** "Sama was a Kinnari on the banks of the river Candabhaga. One day when the Buddha Vipassi was wandering about there, she presented him with a bunch of Salala flowers and thereby obtained admission into the Tavatinsa heaven. In this Buddhapada she was born at Kosambi and became friend of Samavati. After the tregical death of this queen she took holy order, but could not obtain tranquility of mind during the first twenty five years after her ordination," (Muller,1893: Introduction, xxi).

Below we give descriptions about the four Theris, as contained in the main text, the Atthakatha, from the translation by William Pruitt.

i. **Theri Citta (Cittā):** Citta too performed meritorious deeds under previous Buddhas and accumulated good deeds in various lives as her basis for release. Ninety-four aeons ago she was born in the womb of a Kinnari on the banks of Chandrabhaga. In this Buddha era she was born in the home of a wealthy householder in Rajagaha. She also remembers that, "At that time I was a Kinnari on the banks of Chandrabhaga. I saw the faultless Buddha, Self-Depending Unconquered," (William Pruitt, 1998: 48-50).

ii. **Theri Punna (Puṇṇā):** Punna performed meritorious deeds under previous Buddhas and accumulated good actions in various lives as her basis during that world period. She was reborn of a kinnari on the bank of the river Chandrabhaga in a world period without a teaching Buddha. In this Buddha era she was born in Savathi in the home of a wealthy householder. She was named Punna, (William Pruitt, 1998: 16-17).

iii. **Another Sama ('Sāmā'):** Theri Sama too did …. At the time of the Blessed One Vipassi, she was reborn in the womb of a kinnari on the bank of Chandrabhaga river, (William Pruitt, 1998: 63-65).

iv. **Dantika (Dantikā):** Theri Dantika too…. At a time without a teaching Buddha she was born in the womb of a kinnari on the banks of Chandrabhaga river. One day while playing and walking about with the kinnaras, she saw a certain Pacceka Buddha seated at the foot of a certain tree as his daytime resting place. Seeing him with, (William Pruitt, 1998: 70-73).

### V. Apadana

Apadana contains stories of about 587 Theras and Theris. They constitute forty Theris and the rest are Theras. The part containing the stories of the Theras is named as Therapadana or Therapadanapali and that containing the stories of the Theris as Theriapadana or Theriapadanapali.

### A. Therapadana:

Kinnaras lived in the Himalaya quite widely. Some of the mountains there, are named as: Asoka, Paduma, Sobhita, Govala, Romasa, Lambaka, Harita, Bhutagana, Nisabha, Kukkara, Gotama, Vasabha, Kukkata, Romasa, etc. The Theras lived in a wider area in the Himalaya but the concentration of their habitation is shown on the banks of river Chandrabhaga. Besides Chandrabhaga, a few of them also lived on the banks of Sindhu, Jhelum (Vitasta), in the north-west and Bhagirathi in the Central Himalaya. Some also lived near the lake Anotatta (Mansarovar).

About three dozen Theras give reference to Himavanta, Himalaya, as having lived there. Reference to Chandrabhaga is made by about one and half a dozen times. There lived one monk on the river Jhelum (Vitasta), two on Sindhu, and some three or four on Bhagirathi.

These monks are of two classes. Some tell themselves as Kinnara and Kinnari and the others are not Kinnaras. According to the stories Kinnara theris or theras were born here and were inhabitants of the place. In the stories each monk tells, 'I was a Kinnara' or 'Kinnari then.' It was one of their former incarnations. The monks while living here had vision of the Buddha as a Bodhisattva. They made offerings to the Lord and received teachings from Him. As a result of their practice of the pure Doctrine according to the teachings of the Master they were delivered from the life of Kinnara and attained liberation.

#### a. Theras living on the River Chandrabhaga, not Kinnaras

The following theras lived on the banks of the river Chandrabhaga. But they don't tell that they are Kinnaras.

i. Timirapupphiya (366), ii. Timirapupphiya (81), iii. Yūthikapupphiya (167), iv. Macchadāyaka (266), v. Tīṇuppalamāliya (339) and vi. Ekachattiya (409).

**b. Kinnara Theras living on the banks of river Chandrabhaga:**

There lived Theras on the banks of the river Chandrabhaga. They tell that once in their earlier life they were born in the life of Kinnara and they were living on the banks of river Chandrabhaga. They are:

i. Candanapūjaka (133), ii. Saḷalapupphiya (268), iii. Salaḷapupphiya (367) and iv. Ajjunapupphiya (513).

**B. Theriapadana: Kinnari Theris living on the banks of river Chandrabhaga**

According to the Theriapadana the following three Theris were living on the banks of river Chndrabhaga. They call themselves as Kinnari. They were living there in the life of Kinnari. There they had the vision of the visit of the Great Lorḍ. They offered their reverence in their own way. As a result of their pious work they attained liberation from the life of Kinnari and freedom from the act of rebirth. They are:

i. Tīṇinaḷamālikā (5), ii. Salalapupphikā (12) and iii. Sālamālikā (16).

Thus we find that there lived Theris and Theras, who call themselves as Kinnari and Kinnara, in one of their former lives, on the banks of the river Chandrabhaga. This suggests that there in the valley of the river Chandrabhaga at its head, which today is known as Lahul, there lived Kinnaras. The inhabitants of the valley of Chandrabhaga were known as Kinnara.

These accounts also indicate that the inhabitants of the region of the banks of river Chandrabhaga, its headwaters, were given sermons from the Faith and blessed by bringing them into the refuge of the Law.

**1. Therapadana:**

Below we give extracts of the stories of some monks living on the Himalaya. Stories about the Kinnara Thera and Theris who have been living on the banks of river Chandrabhaga are given in more detail.

**a. Theras living on the Himalaya mountains – Some Features:**

**Features:** Below we give description as to how the monks lived on the Himalaya, viz. their residence, dress, food, etc. The number in brackets after the names of the monks indicate the serial number given by Walters in his works.

i. **Food:** Biḷālidāyaka (109) dwelt in the Himalayan region. "Not feeling any greed for food, I was always happy back then digging up roots like kaḷamba, biḷāli and takkaḷ. I ate them prepared by adding jujube." Subhuti (21) says, "At that time I was not eating fruits and roots and freshly picked leaves. I was always subsisting the stuff that fell into my bowl." He lived on the offerings made by the people. The normal diet of the monks living on the Himalaya was fruits, roots and freshly gathered plants and leaves.

ii. **Dress**: Raṃsisaññaka (86-2) living on a Himalayan mountain was a bark-clothed ascetic. Raṃsisaññika (85) lived on a Himalayan mountain and was wearing a deer-leather for outer robes. Phaladāyaka (87) lived on a Himalayan mountain, wearing a rough deer-leather robe.

iii. **Shelters:** Subhuti (21) lived on the Nishabha mountain. He had a ashram well-constructed of leaves. Ekachattiya (409) says that while living on Candabhāgā River's bank, he had a well-made hermitage. It was strewn with very white sand, and furnished with halls made of leaves, Saddasaññaka (88) lived on a mountain in the Himalaya and while dwelling there he used mat of leaves. Biḷālidāyaka (109) in the Himalayan region dwelt also on a mat made of leaves. Mettagu (400) lived on the mountain named Asoka. His hermitage was constructed by Vissakakamma i.e. Visvakarma, the god of the craftsmen and architects. His hut might have been worked by a highly skilled craftsman, with high elaboration.

iv. **Kinds of offerings:** The monks made offerings to the Buddha of fruits, flowers, etc. Padumuttara, Culla Panthaka (92) offered floral umbrella to the Lord. Phaladāyaka (87), with fruit in hand, saw the Buddha and offered the fruit to the Lord and became famous as Phaladayaka, fruit-giver.

v. **Tasks of the Theras:** In the Ashram they had number of students and they taught them. Pupphathūpiya (122) says that, "In the Himalayan region there's a mountain named Lambaka. I was dwelling at its center, a brahmin master of mantras. At that time five thousand students were constantly surrounding me. They all rose earlier than I, and were likewise skilled in mantras."

The following is an example of a general description of a Thera living on the Himalaya mountain:

**Padapūjaka (296):**

On a Himalayan mountain,
I was a kinnara back then.
I saw the Buddha, Stainless One,
bright but cool like a rayless sun

who had approached me at that time,
Vipassi Buddha, World-Leader.
And then I rubbed upon his feet
sandalwood and also incense.

The supplicant says that, "I have done what the Buddha taught," (Walters, 2018-1: 388-89).

**b. Theras living on the Lakes**

i. Upāgatabhāsaniya (269) says that amidst the Himalayan mounts there was a well-apportioned lake. "I was a demon (Rakshas) in that place, with low morals, terrifying. Vipassi, Leader of the World, Merciful, Compassionate One, did come into my presence then, with a desire to lift me up."

   This lake may be identified with Rakkhitatala, the sister lake of Anotatta.

ii. **Lake Anotatta:** Theravadana tells that the Buddha delivered a discourse at the lake Anotatta to the assembly of monks which is entitled as 'Rags of Previous Karma' (387). Lake Anotatta, Mansarovar, is situated on the Kailash mountain. It is told as:

Near the lake called Anotatta,
on the lovely level rock ground,
where sparkled gems of different sorts
and varied perfumes filled the woods,

surrounded by the Assembly
of monks, the Leader of the World,
while seated there, did then explain
the former deeds done by himself:

Hear from me, O monks, the karma
which formerly was done by me.

Endowed with all superpowers, in front of the monks' Assembly, at the great Lake Anotatta, thus indeed the Blessed One spoke this short discourse on dharma revealing his own previous conduct, the Buddha-apadāna named "Rags of Previous Karma."

The karmic actions were like lying, murder, etc. and the fruits were like fierce slandering, transmigration to the hell, etc., (Walters, 2018-I: 492 ).

**c. Theras living on the sides of Rivers:**

**i. Sindhu River - Kandalīpupphiya (319):**

Kandalipupphiya lived on the Sindhu river. His descriptions are:

I was a farmer at that time
on the banks of River Indus.
Bound in service to another,
I looked not for that other's rice.

Wandering along the Indus,
I saw Siddhattha, the Victor,
sitting down in meditation
like a lotus flower in bloom.

I having cut off all the stems
of seven plantain flowers then,
did spread them out upon the head
of Buddha, Kinsman of the Sun, (Walters, 2018-I: 408).

**ii. Vitasta (Jhelum) River - Sudassana (132):**

Sudassana lived on the Vitasta (Jhelum) river. (Kashyap reads Vinatā). He tells his story in the following words:

On the Vitattha River's bank,
there was a fig tree bearing fruit.
While I was searching for that tree
I saw the Leader of the World.

Seeing a pandanus in bloom,
after having cut off a stalk,
I gifted it to the Buddha,
Sikhi, the Kinsman of the World.

"Whatever knowledge you've attained of the eternal, deathless state, I sing that knowledge's praises, O Best Buddha, O Sage so Great. Doing pūjā thus for knowledge, I then saw the fruiting fig tree; I have obtained that perception: that's the fruit of knowledge-pūjā. In the thirty-one aeons since I offered that flower to him. I've come to know no bad rebirth: that's the fruit of knowledge-pūjā. I have done what the Buddha taught, (Walters, 2018-I: 253).

**iii. Bhagirathi river:**

*i.* **Phaladāyaka (305):** At that time on the bank of the river Bhāgīrathī there was a hermitage. Once he went to that hermitage, with an expectation holding a fruit in his hands. He saw Vipassi Buddha there, bright but cool like a rayless sun. He donated to the Teacher all of the fruit he had in his hands. In the ninety-one aeons since he gave that fruit to him, he says, he has come to know no bad rebirth: that is the fruit of giving fruit, (Walters, 2018-I: 395 ).

*ii.* **Khadiravaniya Revata (9):** The River named Bhāgīrathī is fed by the Himalayas. I, a Boatman on the near bank, ferried folks over the rough ford. "The Lord named Padumuttara the Sambuddha, the Best Biped, with one hundred thousand arahants will need to cross the raging stream." Getting many boats tied as one very carefully by workers and having made a covering, I honored him, the Bull of Men. When the Sambuddha had arrived he then climbed onto that large boat. In the middle of the river the Teacher spoke these verses then, (Walters, 2018-I: 82).

*iii.* **Dhotaka (401):** The River named Bhāgīrathī is fed by the Himalayas. It is always flowing along, past the gate of Haṃsavatī. The hermitage named Sobhita, well-built, is on the river's slopes. The Buddha, Padumuttara, the World's Leader, was dwelling there. He was honored by the people, like Indra by the thirty gods. The Blessed One was seated there fearlessly just like a lion. I was a brahmin living in the city of Haṃsavatī. My name back then was Chalaṇga, named thus because I was a sage, (Walters, 2018-I: 595).

**d. The City of Haṃsavatī:**

i. The river named Bhagirathi is fed by the Himalayas. It is always flowing along past the gate of Haṃsavatī, (Walters, 2018-I: 595).

ii. One hundred thousand aeons hence Padumuttara was the Sage. The city named Haṃsavatī was the home of that Buddha's clan. Ganges River always flows past the gate of Haṃsavatī, (Walters, 2018-II: 156).

Like the banks of Chandrabhaga the city of Hamsavati also appears to have been very important. Several Theras and Theris were born and lived here. Kashyap (ed.) in his work Apadana in Devanagari script reads it as Hasavati. The reading Haṃsavatī appears to be a better reading. Many of the Theris revere Padumuttara who is said to be living in the city.

**e. Theras living on the River Chandrabhaga, not Kinnaras:**

The following Theras lived on the banks of the river Chandrabhaga. But they don't tell that they are Kinnaras.

**i. Timirapupphiya (366)**

On Candabhāgā River's bank,
I was going with the current.
I saw the Spotless One, Buddha,
like a regal sal tree in bloom.

Happy, with pleasure in my heart,
taking a timira flower
to the Supreme Pacceka-Sage,
I strew it on that Buddha's head.
In the ninety-one aeons
since I did pūjā with that flower,
I've come to know no bad rebirth:
that's the fruit of Buddha-pūjā, (Walters, 2018-I: 470-71).

It says that the Thera while going along the river saw the Buddha, the Spotless One. He offered the timira flower to the Buddha. As a result of the Puja with that flower he experienced and attained the special knowledge of life and gained complete deliverance. Other legends relating to Chandrabhaga give similar descriptions.

ii. **Timirapupphiya (81):** Timirapupphiya while living on the bank of the river Chandrabhaga was going along the stream when he saw the Monk sitting there, the Brilliant One, the Unperturbed. Having pleased his heart about him he thought in this way at that time: "he who has achieved nirvana will make others achieve nirvana. After reflecting in this way then picking up a dark flower he laid it on top of the head of Siddhattha the Sage so Great," (Walters, 2018-I: 198).

iii. **Yūthikapupphiya (167):** Travelling along the bank of the river Chandrabhaga the Thera saw the Self-Become-One there, like a regal sal tree in bloom. Carrying a jasmine flower, he approached the Sage so Great. Happy, with pleasure in his heart, he gave the Buddha that flower, (Walters, 2018-I: 286 ).

iv. **Macchadāyaka (266):** On Chandrabhaga River's bank Macchadayaka was a bird preying fish. At that time he brought a big fish and gave it to the Buddha named Siddhattha, (Walters, 2018-I: 365).

v. **Tīṇuppalamāliya (339):** The monk Tiṇuppalamaliya then in the life of a monkey was living on the bank of the river Chandrabhaga. At that time he saw the Stainless Buddha who was seated on a mountainside. He was enraptured seeing him, shining forth in all directions, like a regal sal tree in bloom, bearing the great and lesser marks. Happy, with his heart exultant, and his mind bristling with joy, he offered on the Buddha's head three lovely blue lotus flowers, (Walters, 2018-I: 447).

vi. **Ekachattiya (409):**

On Candrabhaga River's bank,
I had a well-made hermitage.
It was strewn with very white sand,
and furnished with halls made of leaves.
The river there was beautiful,
with flat banks and good bathing fords.
It was full of fish and turtles:
crocodiles resorted to it, (Walters, 2018-I: 650-51).

The description is quite long. It describes the environment of the hermitage giving in detail names of various kinds of vegetation and fauna.

### f. Kinnara Theras living on the banks of river Chandrabhaga:

There lived Theras on the banks of the river Chandrabhaga. They tell that once in their earlier life they were born in the life of Kinnara and they lived on the banks of river Chandrabhaga.

**i. Candanapūjaka (133):**

On Candabhāgā River's bank,
I was a kinnara back then.
I lived on flowers as my food
and dressed in clothes made of flowers.

The Wise One, Great Intelligence,
having descended from the sky,
[and] spreading out his upper robe sat
on it, legs crossed together.

Carrying [some] sandalwood oil,
I went to the Victor's presence.
Happy, with pleasure in [my] heart,
I gave [that oil] to the Buddha.

In the eighteen hundred aeons
since I did sandalwood-pūjā,
I've come to know no bad rebirth:
that's the fruit of Buddha-pūjā, (Walters, 2018-1:254-55).

**ii. Saḷalapupphiya (268):**

On Candabhāgā River's bank
I was a kinnara back then.
I saw the Buddha, Vipassi,
Surrounded by a Net of Rays.

Happy, with pleasure in my heart,
and filled with supreme joyfulness,
taking a saḷala flower, I strew it before Vipassi.
He experienced no bad birth since a number of births,
(Walters, 2018-1:367).

**iii. Salaḷapupphiya (367):**

On Candabhāgā River's bank
I was a kinnara back then.
And then I saw the God of Gods,
Bull of Men, walking back and forth.

Plucking a salaḷa flower,
I gave it to the Buddha.

The Great Hero, the Buddha sniffed
that divinely-scented flower, (Walters, 2018-1: 471).

**iv. Ajjunapupphiya (513):**

On Candabhāgā River's bank,
I was a kinnara back then.
I saw the Buddha, Stainless One,
the Self-Become, Unconquered One.

Happy, with pleasure in my heart,
awe-struck, with hands pressed together,
taking an arjuna flower,
I worshipped the Self-Become One.
Due to that karma done very well,
with intention and firm resolve,
leaving my kinnara body,
I went to Tāvatiṃsa then, (Walters, 2018-I: 829).

**2. Theri-apadana: Kinnari Theris living on the banks of river Chandrabhaga**

According to the Theriapadanapali the following three Theris were living on the banks of river Chndrabhaga. They call themselves as Kinnari. They were living in the life of Kinnari. There they had vision of the visit of the Lord of the Lords to the place. They offered their reverence in their own way. As a result of their pious work they attained liberation from the life of Kinnari and freedom from the act of rebirth.

**i. Tīṇinaḷamālikā (5):**

On the Candrabhaga river's bank
I was a kinnarī back then.
I saw the Stainless Buddha there,
Self-Become, the Unconquered One.

Happy, with pleasure in my heart,
awe-struck, with hands pressed together,
taking a garland made of reeds,
I worshipped the Self-Become, (Walters, 2018-II: 11).

Thus Tīṇinaḷamālikā herself tells that she was a Kinnari in one of her earlier lives and was residing on the banks of river Chandrabhaga. There she visioned the Stainless Buddha. With great honour she offered him a garland made of reeds. As a result of that good karma done she took birth in the lands of the gods.

She in the world of thirty-three gods, where there lived thirty-three kings of gods, was placed in the seat of the chief queen. Then in the world of ten kings, who were all wheel-turners, she was fixed in the chief queen's place. All her defilements were now burnt up. She is now elated that now there will be no more rebirth. She has experienced in the ninety-four aeons since she did pūjā with that flower, she has come to know of no bad rebirth. That's the fruit of Buddha-pūjā. All her new existences are destroyed. 'Like elephants with broken chains, I am living without constraint,' she says.

**ii. Salalapupphikā (12):**

On Candabhāgā River's bank,
I was a kinnarī back then.
And then I saw the God of Gods,
Bull of Men, walking back and forth.

Plucking a salala flower, I gave it to the Best Buddha.
And then the Great Hero did sniff the salala
with divine scent. Accepting it the Sambuddha,
Vipassi, Leader of the World,
Great Hero then sniffed it again
for me while I was watching him
Pressing my hands together then,
I worshipped the Best of Bipeds. (Walters, 2018-1I:26).

As a result of this she gained liberation from the cycle of birth and death.

**iii. Sālamālikā (16):**

On Candabhāgā River's bank,
I was a kinnarī back then.
I saw the Stainless One, Buddha,
the Self-Become, Unconquered One.
Happy, with pleasure in my heart,
awe-struck, with hands pressed together,
taking a salala-flower garland,
I worshipped the Self-Become One.

Due to that karma done very well,
with intention and firm resolve,
discarding my human body,
I went to Tāvatiṃsa then, (Walters, 2018-II: 34).

As a result of this good deed she gained liberation from the cycle of birth and death.

Thus we find that there lived Theris and Theras, who call themselves as Kinnari and Kinnara, in one of their former lives on the banks of the river Chandrabhaga, the present region of Lahul, situated at the headwaters of the river.

The above account has been given from the Apadana given in English translation by Jonathan Walters. Jagdish Kashyap has edited a different set of Apadana in Pali. We give here matter from the same:

**a. Therapadana: The following theras lived on the banks of Chandrabhaga:**

1. Uttiya thera (I-3-8-93), Candabhāgānadī tīre susumāroahaṃ.
2. Macchdāyaka, (I-27-6-281). Candabhāgānadī tīre ukkasoāsahaṃ tadā.
3. Javahaṁsaka, (I-27-7-282), Candabhāgānadī tīre āsiṃ vancaro tadā.
4. Billiya, (II-45-3-26), Candabhāgānadī tīre assmosuketo mama.
5. Saḷalapupphiya, (I-27-8-282), Candabhāgānadī tīre ahosim kinnro tadā.
6. Ajjunapupphiya, (II-52-6-92), Candabhāgānadī tīre ahosim kinnro tadā.

These are six theras who tell that they lived on the banks of Chandrabhaga. Two of them nos. 5 & 6, tell that they were kinnaras. They introduce themselves with the common sentence as, Candabhāgānadī tīre ahosiṃ kinnaro tadā. Others, nos. 1-4, don't say that they were kinnaras. They give each a different statement.

**b. Theriapadana:**

1. Naḷamālikā, (II-1-5-184). Candabhāgānadī tīre āhosiṃ kinnarī tadā. These all the three theris write the same sentence.
2. Saḷalpupphikā, (II-2-2-194).
3. Naḷamālikāpupphikā, (II-2-6-199).

All the three theris write one common sentence stating that they were kinnaris and lived on the banks of river Chandrabhaga. On comparison we find some difference in the two editions both in number and names of the theras and theris.

**Archaeology of the High Himalaya**

i. Archaeologists from India, China and other countries are working to discover the secrets of the ancient past of the inhabitants of the High Himalaya. The team lead by Vinod Nautiyal (2014) have examined some burial places in Lippa, Kanam, etc. in Kinnaur, Himachal Pradesh. They have also studied the border villages like Malari in Uttrakhand. A skeleton of a child has also been excavated in Spiti and is presently preserved in the State Museum, Shimla. Archaeologists have excavated and discovered valuable findings from Mustang in Nepal. The most important of all these is a gold burial mask excavated in Guge in Tibet.

ii. **The Guge Burial Gold Mask:** There are two gold masks excavated by the archaeologists from Guge. Yeshe Rabphel Ritro gives remarks on them:

  a. Yeshe Rabphel Ritro writes, "This intricately designed golden burial mask was unearthed in Chuthak (Chu-thags), Guge. This object is 3.5 cm. in height. Like Gurgyam specimen the Chuthak mask was discovered in the Satlej valley drainage system; the two sites are not more than 120 kms. distant from one another. The Chuthak mask also appears to be fashioned from gilt silver plates. Note the engraved zoomorphic motifs (birds and caprids), tiered structures of the upper plate. Photo courtesy of Lin Luhui, the archaeologist who discerned exceptionally important Tibetan cultural artifact in 2011. Linhui estimates that the Chuthag mask is around 2,000 years old." Thus we may place it in around 1st century C.E.

  b. On the other finding Rotro remarks, "The long straight, narrow nose depicted on the Gurgyam mask is intriguing. Also the eyes of Gurgyam mask are more round than they were of a pair having the epicanthic folds of east Asians. The face portrayed seems to have Caucasian features, as represented among Indian and Eurasian population. I have made some of these

> observations for the elaborate burial masks recently discovered in Chuthak. Nonetheless, these observations on the anatomical element of the Tibetan masks are unverified in themselves," (Yeshe Rabphel Rotro, 1914, Internet, retrieved on Jan. 19, 2023).

The mask described first wears a crown like a cap but it appears to be quite loose. As such we may consider it as more a decorative object like crown than of utility. The carvings are of a wild animal like deer, birds and plants, with a flower about to bloom.

# 3

# Kinnaras in History and Art

### Kimpurushas

Scholars maintain that Kimpurusha and Kinnara are the same people and the Kinnaras were formerly known as Kimpurusha. Literally both the words in Sanskrit mean the same as'What Man?'

Kimpurusha is said to be found mentioned first in the Yajurveda. Dowson describes the term as 'An indescribable man; one of a low type, partaking of the nature and appearance of animals. In later times it is synonymous with Kinnara.' S.K. Chatterji quoting from the Yajurveda, where they are recorded for the first, writes that "Kimpurusha was then described as an ugly man, a wild man, an ape," (Chatterjee: 1974: 27). Like the Kirata and others they were offered in the man-offering sacrifices for the mountains. Thus it may be said that they lived in the mountains.

During the Puranic period they constituted a large population. Atkinson writes that Agnihotra, according to the Vishnu Purana, divided Jambudwipa into nine portions among his nine sons. The division of the Kimpurushas was known as Kumpurushvarsha. Similarly in the Matsya Purana, in the division of Jambudvipa, the continent, into seven varshas or divisions, one was named as Kimpurshvarsha, the land of the Kimpurushas, (Agrawal, 1963: 186). The inhabitants were known as such. Both the Puranas give the same geographical position. North of it lay the mountain range of Hemakuta and in the south lay Himavan, the Himalaya, and south of it lay Bharatavarsha. From this it may be understood that Kimpurpurushas lay beyond the Himalaya, but actually in the Himalaya. Rahul Sankrityayan suggests western Himalaya.

Alberuni writes that the river Ganges which is the middle and main stream flows through Kalapagrama, i.e. the city of the most virtuous

Kimpurusha. Alberuni here gives the proper location of the habitat of the Kimpurushas.

### Kinnara and Kimpurusha

Kinnaras, whether mythical or historical, are generally shown as mountaineers living in the Himalayas. S.M. Ali writes, quoting from the Puranas that "The inhabitants of the Himalaya are Kinnars," (S.M. Ali, 1966: 58). "At several places on these mountains there are the cities of Kinnaras, which are in the central part of the many-peaked Himalaya about one hundred in number." D C Sircar considers the Kimpurshas and Kinnaras as Himalayan people. They are both mountaineers living in the Himalayas.

Matsya Purana, gives description about the inhabitants of Kimpurushavarsha as that, "The people of Kimpurusha-Khanda have a complexion like that of heated gold, and they live upto 10,000 years. A stream of honey flows from a Plaksa tree, in that sacred Khanda which the Kinnaras residing there drink. On account of which they remain so healthy, without any grief, and happy, and cheerful on their minds. The people have a yellow complexion like shining gold and the women folk are known as Apsaras," (Taluqdar, 1916:310). Here the inhabitants of Kimpurusha khanda may be naturally called Kimpurushas. But here they are also called Kinnara. Thus according to the Matsya Purana Kimpurushas and the Kinnaras are the same people.

Rahul Sankrityayan writes that at sometime earlier the whole of western Himalaya might have been named as Kimpurushavarsha, where there lived the Kimpurushas or Kinnaras. Thus the territorial expansion of the Kinnara inhabitants was much wider.

### Kinnaras and Asvamukhi

Distinguishing between the Kinnara and Kimpurusha, Upadhyaya writes, "Kinnaras were supposed to possess a human head and the body of horse. Such specimens in sculptures are preserved in Muttra Museum. Another kind of them was that which bore the head of a horse and the body of a human being. Females of this type have been alluded to by Kalidasa in his phrase asvamukhyah. The Asvamukhi Jataka contains a story of such a being which finds itself carved in many railing pillars of the Kusana times. Like Gandharvas they are also described as celestial minstrels. They are otherwise called Kimpurushas," (Upadhayaya, 1947:

318). Upadhyaya describes Kimpurushas of two kinds and females as Asvamukhi. And proposing that Kimpurushas are also 'Asvamukhya,' they are horse-headed. Upadhayaya quotes in reference a Jataka named Asvamukhi Jataka. It may be clarified that Asvamukhi or Assamukhi Jataka is not available for reference in the collection of Jatakas.

In this regard Coomarswamy writes, "A Yakkhini by name, or rather, epithet, Assa-mukhi (horse-faced) plays an important part in the Padakusalamanava Jataka. There may be specific reference to this Jataka whenever a horse-headed Yakkhini is represented on the medallions of Buddhist railings. But the Kinnaras and Kimpurusas, and Gandharvas too, typically half-human, half-equine, are a class of beings frequenting forests and mountains (cf. the valava-mukha Cetiya) and as such are sometimes naturally represented as a part of the scenery, and in such cases there need be no reference to the Jataka," (Coomarswamy, 1931-I: 10).

Following Coomarswamy, we find that in the Jataka No. 432 a Yakkhini is described with horse-headed but the rest having human body. The story runs that, "Once upon a time in the reign of Brahmadatta, king of Benaras, his queen-consort after falling in sin was questioned and taking a vow she said, "If I have sinned against you, I shall become a female Yakkha with a face like a horse." After her death she became a horse-faced Yakkha and dwelt in a rock-cave in a vast forest at the foot of a mountain, (Cowell, Padakusalamanava Jataka No. 432). Coomarswamy identified this figure in a carving by associating it with this Jataka. This Assamukhi Yakkha is a singular example. There are also a few similar Yakshis in the Jataka. But they do not form a class. This figure in the carvings is distinguishable from those of Kinnaras who have a distinct form and role of their own class. Kimpurusha is a rare subject in art.

### Kinnaras in Art

We observe Kinnaras depicted in the pictures in different aspects. But little is known about the pictures of Kimpurushas in art. However, in the literature there is drawn some distinction between the figures of Kinnara and Kimpurushas in respect of their presentation in the pictures. This perhaps does not apply to their human forms. Panchmukhi writes, "Though the lexicons equate Kinnara with Kimpurusha, the *Vachaspatya* draws a distinction between the two on the basis of literary evidences. The Kimpurusha has the hips of horse and the face of man, while Kinnara has the horse face and human body," (Panchmukhi, 1951:25-26). This is a subject of art.

Kinnaras are described as celestial musicians. In iconography they appear as musicians playing vina, lute, but their figure is depicted variously. A scholar defines the term that, "Kinnara are human beings with horse's heads who form the band of that of Kuvera." Vogel writes in his Indian Serpent Lore that, "Kinnara is a class of fabulous beings represented with the upper half of a human body and the lower half that of a bird." Some scholars presume that the "Gandharvas and Kinnaras are fictitious creatures."

Panchmukhi in his study on the Gandharavas and Kinnaras writes that "Kinnaras and Gandharavas play significant part in the Indian temples." In the ancient literature Kinnaras are described as celestial minstrels playing on Vina, lute. They are seen in the carvings having human-head and lower limbs of horse. Some scholars describe them otherwise also and are seen in the carvings also as such.

Bhattacharya describes the iconographical attributes of the Kinnara king as: "Allied to the Yaksa are the Kinnaras, Gandharvas, and Vidyadharas. They are all semi-mythical beings next to gods, who have power to confer benefit when propitiated. Some information about their kings is found in the Dharmadhatuvagisvara Mandala in the Nispannayogavali. Name of the Kinnara king is not named here but his form is given in the following words: 'The Kinnara king is reddish white in colour and is engaged in playing on the musical instrument called Vina," (Bhattacharyya, 1968: 380).

Kinnara is less known term in Tibetan literature which is translated from Sanskrit as mi-'m-chi, (= whether a man or what?). The same position exists in the art forms. We quote here two references on iconography of Tibetan Buddhism. Kuvera or Vaisravana, God of Wealth, is guardian of the North. "His abode was Alaka in the Himalayas, abounding in wealth and magnificence, where he was attended by the Yaksas and horse-headed man called Kinnaras," (Getty, 1928: 156). "Here Kinnara are described as heavenly musicians, are usually playing lute (vina)," writes Gordon.

Shukla, L.K., gives quite a different and detailed description about the Kinnara: "Kinnara also go with Ghandharvas, but unlike Gandharvas they are characterized by hybridity. According to the Mana [Mansar], 'His legs are like those of an animal, the upper part of the body is that of a man, the face is like that of Garuda and the arms are provided with wings. He is adorned with diadem and red lotus, has the beautiful hue of a flower and holds a lute (Vina)," (L.K. Shukla, 1972: 262). In a different classical work the description is more complex. It clarifies certain carvings with better details. There are carvings with such descriptions. Shukla also distinguishes between the figures of Kinnaras and Gandharvas or Vidyadharas who have entire human body.

Quintanilla describes a sculpture of the Kinnaras as follows: "Immediately flanking the stùpa is a pair of hovering kinnaras who bring offerings of garlands to the stùpa. They have human male heads and torsos, but the wings, claws and tail feathers of a bird," (Quintanilla, 2007:40). This describes the form and functions of Kinnara having a slightly complex figure. In another case Quintanilla states that, 'there are two winged Kinnaras making offerings to the Stupa, both at the foremost of the row on both the sides of the stupa.'

"A fragmentary relief depicting a flying kinnara bringing offerings to a sacred site, indicated by the remains of a chattra, may also be attributed to the late second century B.C.E." However, this kinnara may be included among sculptures of the late second century B.C.E. because of the increased softness of his form, the looped sash, the turban type, and the glimmer of expression in his face, legs of animal, winged, human body," (Quintanilla, 2007: 40). The figures appear to follow the descriptions of Shukla. We also learn about the period of the carvings.

Their carvings appear at Amravati, Sanchi, Bharhut, etc. They are seen flying and also standing erect. They appear playing on musical instruments and offering flowers to the deities or sacred objects. Kinnaras were a popular subject in the carvings.

# 4

# Kinnaras: Different Names and the Historical People

## 1. Kinnaras: Different Names

The Pali literature records that there lived Kinnaris and Kinnaras on the banks of river Chandrabaga, the valley of the river which presently is named as Lahul. This indicates that the people living in the upper valley of Chandrabhaga were once known as Kinnara, as also noticed above, (Tobdan, 2022: 101-152).

Dipavansa referring to the occasion when the missionaries in c. 250 B.C.E. were sent to the Himalayas in the time of the emperor Asoka, designates the inhabitants of the whole of the Himalaya with one epithet as 'Yakkha' or 'Yaksha.' It writes, "The Thera who originated from the Kassapa tribe, Majjhima, Durabhisara, Sahadeva, Mulakadeva converted the multitude of Yakkhas in the Himavata. They preached there the Suttanta, called Dhammacakkapavattana," (Oldenberg, 1879:159). Thus now all the inhabitants of the Himalya are known by one term as Yaksha. This includes also the inhabitants of the the banks of river Chandrabhaga who sometime after are called as Kinnara. The Kinnaras were first known as Kimpurushas and then became Kinnara and now they are designated as Yaksha.

In the ruins of a monastery at the famous Buddhist site at Nagarjunikonda an inscription was discovered. It refers to the same instance of sending the missionaries in c. B.C.E. 250 to different countries including the Himalayas, by the emperor Asoka for the propagation of the Dhamma. It records the details nearly complete as given in the two ancient Ceylonese works of Dipavansa and Mahavansa. In the description about the Himalaya we observe a slight change. This may be taken as the thought and the view prevailing then at the time of installation of the structures about the people of the Himalayas.

This inscription was studied by Vogel and later also by D.C. Sircar and Lahiri. Sircar and Lahiri date the inscription to c. middle of the third century C.E., (Sircar and Lahiri, Epi. Ind. Vol. XXXIII: 247-250). Vogel notes that, "The shrine is stated to have been dedicated to the fraternities of Ceylonese monks who had converted Kashmir, Gandhara, Chīna, Chilāta (= Skt. Kirāta), Tosāli, Avaramta (Skt. – Apranta), ….." (Vogel, Epi. Indica, XX:1933: 7-8, 22-23). It has been clarified here that Chilāta stands for Kirāta. The two names Cīna and Kirāta between Gandhar and Tosali stand undoubtedly for the people and the regions inhabited by them representing the whole Himalaya. The Himalaya here is divided into two parts west and east. The people living in the west are designated as Cīna and those on the east as Kirāta. Here the term Chīna stands for Kinnara.

The same two names – Cīna and Kirāta – appear in the work of Varahamihira together. The Kiratas and Cinas are seen mentioned together by B.C. Law as, "The powerful ruler of Pragjyotish (Kamrupa) led a mighty Maleccha army of Kirāta and Cīna in the battle of Kurukshetra,' (Law, B.C. 1943:282). That the Himalaya was divided in two parts as west and east, in respect of the kind of its population, inhabited respectively by the Kinnaras and the Kiratas, is also explained by Rahul Sankrityayan. Rahul writes that, "at one time the country of the Kinnaras in the Himalaya extended from the headwaters of Ganga to the west upto the headwaters of Satluj and Chandrabhaga. The Kiratas lived from the headwaters of Ganga upto Nepal," (Rahul, 1953: 42). This is an explanation of the subject contained in the inscription of Nagarjunikonda and some other sources, as above, that when the Himalaya is divided into two parts, on the west live the Kinnaras and on the east live the Kiratas.

It is notable that the Asoka's missionaries sent to different regions for the propagation of the Dhamma belonged to Ceylon, Sri Lanka.

Thus we see that the same people as Kinnara were first known as yaksha, then they were known as Kinnara and now as Chīna. Before this, in the earliest period, they were known as Kimpurusha. So it is difficult to recognise a people in history only by one name.

We also read another instance as follows. B.C. Law writes about the Kiratas that, "They are referred to in the Mahabharata (XII, 207, 43) together with Yuanas or Yavanas, Kambojas, …..", (Law, 1943:282). Further S.M. Ali writes, "According to the Puranic cosmography, Bharatavarsa was divided into nava khandas, or nine divisions or units. The ninth khanda extends for 1,000 yojanas. On the east live Kiratas, on its west, Yavanas," (Ali, 1966: 127). Here in the territorial division of the land the Kiratas are shown to live in the east. On the other end, in the west, live Yavanas. We don't know with whom the Yavanas here should be identified.

## 2. Kinnara Kings

**Kinnara King from the Purana:** Mankad cites name of a king from the Vayu Purana named as a 'Kinnara'. Whether it is a personal name or it represents a tribe cannot be decided. He writes, "Starting from the close of the Mahabharata war, we get the following genealogy of the Solar line in different Puranas," (Mankad, 1951: 48). The name is not found in the other Puranas named here as Visnu, Matsya, Bhagwan, Bhavishya, and Garuda.

"Thereafter he, whose other name was Kinnara and whose exploits were sung by the Kinnaras, the son of Vibhisana, became the ruling chief of the men," (, 1-197:31).

**Kinnara King from the Rajatarangini:** Rajatarangini provides that Nara-I also named as Kinnara, son of Vibhishana, was the king of Kashmir. He was an early king. His prowess was sung by the Kinnaras. Though this king followed the right customs, still when the fortune of his subjects turned, he brought about a series of great calamities under the baneful influence of sensuality, (Rajatarangini, i-197). In his time a Buddhist ascetic (Shramana) who was living alone in a Vihara, situated at Kinnaragrama, seduced the [king's] wife through magic power. In his wrath over this the king burned thousands of Viharas, and granted the villages which had belonged to them, to Brahmans residing in Madhyamatha. He built the city of Narapura or Kinnarapura on the banks of Vitasta, Jhelum which was destroyed by the Nagas. He annoyed the Nagas and was destroyed by them.

## 3. Kinnaras: The Living People

As we have seen above historically Lahul, the banks of river Chndrabhaga, was one of the lands where there lived Kinnaras. It was a Kinnarland. Lahul is now changed so much that it is difficult to recognise it as such in one glance. But there certainly exist identities of the historical Kinnaras.

We have attempted to identify the inhabitants of Malana as splinter group of Kinnaras because they have similarities with Kinnaur, ethnic and linguistic. Kinnaur is identified by the modern scholars as Kinnarland in respect of geography, ethnicity and language.

Ancient scholars were broadly aware of the location of the habitation of Kinnaras. Chakladar explains referring to the work of Kalidas that the Kinnaras were different from the Kiratas. They are mentioned in Indian literature along the Yaksas and Gandharvas. Since Raghu, a character in the drama, does not reach Kailash the country of Kinnaras must have been to the west of Kailash and the Manasa. In the Mahabharata also Arjuna during his conquest reaches the country of the Kimpurusha first, the Hatakadesa of Guhyaka and thereafter the Manasa lake. Here Kalidas shows that the Kinnaras were the inhabitants of the high Himalaya. He tells about the Himalaya and the Kinnaras as, "It is the mountain whose sides are silvered with eternal snow, and where the Kinnaras have to walk a road on which the snow had hardened to stone," (Chakladar, 1925: 20). The statement of Chakladar that Kinnaras are different from Kiratas appears to be right. The identification of the habitat of the Kinnaras on the Himalaya on its western part, on the basis of the works of Kalidas and Mahabharata, also appear to be agreeable.

The inhabitants of Kinnaur call themselves as Kanaura and their country as Kanauring. The name, people and the area had attracted attention of the scholars since quite early. The scholars like Rahul, Upadhayaya, Das, etc., firmly assert that the Kanauras of Kinnaur of the upper Satluj valley in Himachal Pradesh are the same as found described in the ancient literature as Kinnara. The inhabitants of Kinnaur have a distinct physical appearance, they speak a language distinct from Indo-Aryan and also Tibetan. It is also allied to the languages of Malana and Lahul. They are the original inhabitants of the place. Geographically also they are not far from the ancient known habitation of the Kinnaras, the banks of Chandrabhaga.

Upadhyaya writes that, "Jayachandra Vidyalankar is correct when he identifies the land of the Kinnaras with modern Kanaur in the upper valley of the Satlej where the headwaters of the Chandrabhaga approach," (Upadhyaya, 1947: 62-note.5).

Das emphatically states that, "Under the circumstances it may not be unjustifiable to identify the Kinnaras of early literature with the modern Kanauris who are the inhabitants of the modern Kanaur valley belonging to the Bashahar state on the bank of the upper Satluj, the land of the Kanauri speaking hilly land which is rugged in an extraordinary degree. The descendants of the old Kinnaras live today in the Kanaur valley extending upto the Shimla hills. They are known today as Kinnauris. They speak a Tibeto-Burmese language closely allied to those of Lahul and Malana. So the Kanauris seem to be the true descendants of devagayakas or svarga-gayakah, i.e. the celetial singers," (Das, 1954: 44-45). Thus there is no doubt that the Kanauris, the inhabitants of the upper Satluj valley, are the descendants of the Kinnaras of the ancient literature.

Rahul Sankritayayan, a great scholar, visited Kinnaur in the summer of 1948, soon after the Independence of the country. He wrote a book entitled as 'Kinnara Deshme,' 'In the country of Kinnaras.' The title of the book itself indicates clearly that the author recognises the area as the country of the Kinnaras. He emphatically writes in the very beginning, while writing on the history of the area that, "This is the country of Kinnaras," (Rauhl, 1948: 291). He further writes that, "In Sanskrit Kimpurush is also used for Kinnara. Therefore it is also called as Kimpurushdesh or Kimpurushvarsha. Kinnara and Kimpurusha were a birth in the life of gods. But we get no help from this in studying history." Thus the areas covering the upper valleys of the rivers Chandrabhaga and the Satluj and the areas nearby are identified as the land of Kinnaras and their inhabitants including the splinter group, the Malanis, are Kinnara, (Tobdan, 2022: 101-152). We have already written in 1984 that the Malanis are a group uprooted from the same area of Kinnaras some time back.

# 5

# Kinnara Malana
# The Kinnaras of Himalaya

**Himalayan Culture**: Himalaya forms a unique, wide and long belt of mountainous land. There have been living here many cultures, generally small, since ancient times, having their own social systems, customs and languages. This distinct cultural zone of the Himalaya might have been earlier much broader. Western Himalaya is stretched and much wider. Here thrived more number of cultures. High precipitous mountain ranges and severe climatic conditions make the movement from one place to another extremely difficult. Yet two long routes, through Kashmir and Kullu-Lahul, forming branches of the great international Silk Route, passed across many high passes through the western Himalaya connecting the two great international cultures of the Indian plains and of the highlands of Central Asia. On it travelled for centuries many cultures and much material was transported.

Himalaya gave birth to many small cultures which, however, remained confined to their areas. In the inner regions amid the High Himalaya there still live some small communities practicing strange cultures and speaking different languages. Malana, a village situated in the remote area of the Malana glen, Parvati valley, Kullu, is one such culture.

## Kanashi: The Language of Malana

The language spoken in Malana is known as Kanashi. This is spoken only in Malana and others cannot understand it. Colin Rosser writes that Kanashi, the language of Malana, differs basically from the dialect of Pahari spoken generally in Kullu. It is stated that, "philologists claim to have found definite links between Malani, Magyar, and Finnish, and that it is also allied – more understandably – to Pharsi." But there is no evidence to prove it.

Other scholars contend that Kanashi has close affinity with Kinnauri, the language of Kinnaur which is situated very near to Malana. Harcourt (1871) gathered some vocabulary of the language and brought its samples before the world. Diack compared words from the language with those from Tibetan, and dialects from Lahul and Kinnauri. He found that Kanashi had affinities with Kinnauri language, (Daick, 1896: 100). He also informs that before him, F.C. Fanshawe published a number of specimens of Kanashi which were observed by W.H. Tribe who noticed that the specimens agreed very closely with the words of the Kinnauri dialect. Thus it is evident that Kanashi has close affinity with Kinnauri.

It is notable that the scientists studying the physical aspects of the people of Malana also arrive at the same conclusion as the linguists. Some early observers remark that the inhabitants of Malana are different in physique from their neighbours. For this reason some scholars believe that they are immigrants from the plains. Harcourt writes that 'the Malauna settlers, the strange people who hold themselves aloof from every one, are a colony driven up from the plains centuries ago.' The following are some detailed observations made by the scholars on the physical aspects of the people of Malana.

Harcourt writes, "The aspect of the males is very peculiar; in stature they are below the middle height, with figures that are far from being well developed: their eyes have a startled look; the nose is without exception long and projecting over the mouth; and this last feature, as does the narrow retreating chin, gives the countenance an imbecile and vacuous expression. Beards and whiskers are, in our acceptation of these terms unknown, and the moustache is hardly perceptible; but the hair is worn long, in elf-like and matted locks. The dress is tattered and the dirty appearance of the men and the few women we saw, renders the villagers of Malauna a far from prepossessing race. The word race is used advisedly, for it is clear these people do not form an integral portion of the inhabitants of Kooloo, and are a distinct species, whose language and social customs do not assimilate with those of the people amongst whom their lot is so strongly cast," (Harcourt, 1870: 41-42).

Gore also observes similar features in the physique of the people of Malana. He writes, "Though they dress much as do the other inhabitants of Kulu, they have quite a different type of face, somewhat Jewish in appearance, with a prominent nose and weak, narrow chin. Their language also is totally distinct which is a proof of their almost complete isolation for some centuries, since it is inconceivable that they could have come from anywhere but from the plains below," (Gore, 1895: 87). In stature, they are thin and moderate in height. Fair in colour and near absence of hair on the face.

Bruce observes that the several young men he saw had exceptionally refined faces, with very clearly cut features though none of them was heavy limbed. He also gives a similar explanation of the ethnic characteristics of the Malanis in the words, "The Malana people are a survival, but a survival of what people it is beyond me to say. Mr. Fitzgerald Lee, in his small guide-book to Kangra district has a short account of this curious fold. He connects their language with ancient Hunnish, and mentions that, on the authority of facts supplied by him, Professor Vambery came to the conclusion that the Malana people were probably a branch of the same family now represented by Turks, Magyars, Finns, etc. This is as it may be, but the features of the best looking of the men resemble the highest Rajput type to my mind," (Bruce, 1914: 177).

The old Gazetteer notes that, "The Kanets of Malana have more refined features than those of the rest of Kulu, which may be due to a separate origin, or to continual in-breeding. They have not been scientifically treated by any anthropologist, but their language has been carefully studied, and points to a mixed aboriginal and Tibetan source. In anyway their race does not give appearance of the group of race to which their language indicates," (Gazetteer 1917-II: 55).

Keeping in view their physical features scholars identify them as not resembling with those living around them. Hence they are presumed to belong to some more distant land. They argue that they are immigrants from the southern direction. But on finding no apparent similar match there also they were presumed as immigrants from some more distant continent. The Malanis are thus equated with Jewish, Hunnish, etc. One much forceful assumption about the inhabitants is that they are the remnants of Alexander's army. But no evidence was coming forth in this regard and may be presumed to be more as a speculation.

Sharma and Bhalla, of the department of Anthropology of the Punjab University, state to have conducted a morphometric study of the Malanis with a view to tracing their relationship with some of their neighbouring populations. It is reported that, "The results show that Malaneese are a distinct population clearly distinguishable from the neighbouring population of Himachal Pradesh. The distance statistics reveal closer morphometric affinity of Malaneese with the Kuluwis and Kinnaura than with Lahulies," (Sharma and Bhalla: Malaneese of Malana Glen, internet source, 18.6.20).

The two scientists reitrate that, 'The Malanis have closer affinity with the Kinnauris than with Lahulis.' Here, it shows that the Malanis are related to the Kinnauris quite closely, who inhabit not very far.

The results of studies of the two scientists that the physiognomy of the Malanis have close relationship with that of the Kinnauris authenticate the observations of the wide range of scholars stating that Kanashi, the language of the Malanis, has close resemblance with Kinnauri. Thus here we observe that on both account, physiognomy and language, Malanis are closely related to the Kinnauris.

Here reference by the two scientists to Lahul is important. Therefore, before placing our view on the findings on the relationship between the Lahulis and Malanis, we may have to consider a point. Constitution of the existing population of Lahul and Kinnaur is the basis of the study. In this respect geography and history of the two regions have played great role.

Kinnaur constitutes almost wholly one longitudinal valley of Satluj. Its northern part joins the Tibetan culture and the lower part the Hill culture of Himachal Pradesh. In this manner its upper and lower parts are affected by these two external cultures. But the middle part which may be more than one third of the whole area of Kinnaur still preserves a good part of its old features. Kinnaur remained mostly peaceful. The population has single entity and it remained generally undisturbed by the external forces, (Tobdan, 2008a). This large region is inhabited by almost one kind of people who speak the same language, with some variations due to geographical reasons, except the small distinct class of the craftsmen who immigrated from the lower regions. Kinnaur remained in the known long historical period generally politically undisturbed. It retains much important aspects of its ancient culture. Scholars affirm that the inhabitants of Kinnaur are the descendants of the Kinnaras of the ancient literature in Pali and Sanskrit, (Tobdan, 2008a: 58). We have also seen above.

Lahul, as we have seen in the previous chapter, was once inhabited by Kinnaras. It may be presumed that the whole population belonged to one ethnic group and spoke one single language. Geographically Lahul consists of three valleys of Chandra, Bhaga and the combined valley of Chandrabhaga. It is bounded on the north and north east by Spiti, Ladakh and Zanskar. They speak the Tibeto-Himalayan languages. On its east and south are situated Bara Bhanghal of Kangra, and Bharmaur and Pangi of Chamba districts. On the west is situated Kullu. They speak Western-Pahari languages. In Lahul there are several doors for immigration to enter: Khoksar from Kunzom and Rohtang, Darcha and Miyar. The biggest route is through the valley of Chandrabhaga from the side of south-west direction, even though the route had been difficult normally for the travellers. Lahul is flanked by the two great international cultures, Central Asian and of the Indian plains, situated on its north and south. A route, a branch of the international Silk Route, passed through Lahul linking the two great cultures and the economic centres of the two regions. Much cultural practices and merchandise goods passed through Lahul, and it kept Lahul exposed to the outside world. Lahulis also had regular annual trip to Western Tibet for trade and also to Kullu for the purpose of trade and winter transmigration.

The three valleys of Lahul are divided into four sections occupied by four distinct societies having defined geographical area and distinct language. In Chandra valley, locally known as Tinan, Tinani is spoken. In sTod, upper Bhaga valley, sTodpa is spoken. In Gahar or Punan, the lower half of the Bhaga valley, Gahari is spoken. In Manchhad, Melogs or Pattan the language spoken is named as Pattani or Songla.

Each geographical-linguistic group was a compact closed society. An inhabitant of one division could not understand the language of the other easily. There was limited social exchange like marriage, etc. till sometime after the independence when the means of communication started expanding. Moreover the size of the population of whole of Lahul was very small. Thus Lahul constitutes a very small society segmented in more than half a dozen totally distinct cultures. The same principle applies to certain extent in the case of ethnology. It presents a complex situation. Taking Lahul as a whole as one single sample for study on any aspect of culture will lead a student to nowhere. Inversely if taken one section for study it will not apply to the whole population. In view of this we cannot say anything about the study of the two scientists as above in respect of Lahul.

In respect of the languages of Lahul, once it was called as the 'Linguistic Paradox.' There are spoken four distinct languages. Although the scholars mention only three. Francke writes in this regard that, "The fact that the little country of Lahoul possesses three distinct languages which are not related to the Aryan languages of India, and only distinctly related to Tibetan has long been a puzzle to philologists," (Francke, 1907: 181). There are at least five distinct language preently spoken in Lahul.

It appears that in Lahul there occurred some great disturbance in the constitution of the societies of the whole of Lahul and that also quite early.

The Linguistic Survey of India takes into consideration the three language of Tinan, Punan and Pattan and all are placed under the Complex Pronomilised languages of the Tibeto-Burman family of languages. They contain the element of Kinnauri. Rahul perhaps was referring to the same element, while speaking about the Kinnaris living on the banks of Chandrabhaga and says that the language is still spoken there.

The findings of the two scientists that the Malanis have affinity with the people of Kinnaur in physiognomy is valuable. It strengthens the results of the studies of the scholars on the language of Malana.

It has been seen that the Malanis have been identified, as above, ethnologically and linguistically, with the Kinnaras of Kinnaur. Therefore there remains no doubt that Malanis too are Kinnaras. Kinnaras had been living in much wider area than Kinnaur.

## Malanis: The Practitioners of Himalayan Culture

There are some other traits found in the cultural practices of Malana about their being the people of the Himalaya.

In Malana clan organization is based on the relationship of bone and in a limited sphere based on milk. Colin Rosser explains the phenomenon, "The only exogamous rule…., the idea being that relatives within seven degrees may not marry. But this only applies to agnatic kinship, regard being paid to the haddi ka natha, not to be dudh ka natha." "While the prohibitive rule within the clan relates to brahmanic marriage rules, the haddi ka natha literally means the relation of bones instead of that of blood. prohibits marriage with the same clan," (Colin Rosser, 1956). This is the cultural practice existing also in Lahul, (Tobdan, 1993:66). This tradition is found also in practice with some small communities living in the high altitude areas of Uttrakhand. The Culture of Malana preserves and practices the traditions of Himalayan Culture. They are the people of the high Himalaya.

**Kanashi: Its Relationship with Tibetan**

It is known that Kanashi in vocabulary contains some words from Tibetan language. Therefore this issue had been intriguing the scholars constantly.

Broad features of Kanashi were gathered quite early. The Gazetteer sums up that, "This Language of Malana glen called Kanashi has no connection with Sanskrit or Hindi, and very little with either the 'Tibetan of Spiti, or the dialects of Lahul, however, that it possesses remarkable affinities with the Kanawari talked in a portion of Rampur-Bashahar State on the Satlaj, and an exhaustive comparison of the two dialects might lead to interesting linguistic and even ethnological discoveries," (Gazetteer 1897-II: 53).

The statement also indicates that Kanashi is not related closely to Tibetan either. Yet Linguists place Kanashi alongwith Kinnauri among the languages of the class of Tibeto-Himalayan languages.

In the Linguistic Survey of India, Grierson places Kanashi under the western sub-group of Complex Pronominalized Languages of the Tibeto-Burman Himalayan group of languages spoken by the inhabitants of the High Himalaya. Grierson further writes that, "Kanashi is apparently closely related to Kanawari, though it makes a less complex impression," (Grierson, 1908: 428). Here Grierson does not appear to be impressed about Kanashi being complex if pronominalised.

The language contains some words from Tibetan and anyhow it was placed among the Tibeto-Himalayan languages. But the amount of Tibetan words in the languge, although important, is very small. The broad basic structure of the language and some other important features of the language have no affinity to Tibetan. It appears that Kanashi and other languages like Kinnauri placed in the same class are in possession of some features which separate them from both the great linguistic families. Thus if these languages do not belong to the class of Indo-Aryan languages they also do not belong to Tibeto-Himalayan. Rahul Sankrityayan appears to place the

Kinnara class of languages in a third and separate category of languages different from both of these two.

Mahapandita Rahul Sankrityayan, a great scholar in Sanskrit, Pali, Tibetan, Hindi, etc., and a great authority on various subjects like Linguistics, Philosophy, History, Religion, etc., discusses in detail the Himalaya, its people and their languages. He writes about Malana, Kinnaur and similar societies in Uttrakhand and their languages like Kinnauri, Kanashi, Raji, etc. and the relationship among them.

Rahul finds that these languages are composed of Sanskrit, Tibetan and a third Language which is independent of these two. He writes that, "both Kinnara (Malani) and Kirata (Raji) languages contain many words from Sanskrit and Tibetan languages. But besides the two, there exists a third language in the form of precipitation," (Rahul, 1953: 42). Here Rahul says that there is a third language in the form of precipitation. Rahul at another place writes that, "Kanauri i.e. Kinnara constitutes a mixture of three languages: Tibetan (Bhoti language), Sanskrit and Kirata. Kirata is different from both of these and may be named as 'Shu'," (Rahul, 1948: 292). Here Rahul recognises the third language as entirely different from the other two and also gives it a name 'Shu' meaning 'god'. The term is drawn from Kinnauri.

Rahul analyzing the Kinnauri language writes again that, "There are three elements in Kinnara language: Basic (Kirata) language, Indo-European (of Sanskrit family) language and Bhot (Tibetan) language," (Rahul, 1948: 376). Further on he calls the third language as the basic language of Kinnauri. Rahul also writes that Kinnara and Raji i.e. Kiratai are branches of the same language, (Rahul, 1958: 23). Here we can add Kanashi also and read Kinnara for Kirata.

Thus according to Rahul Kanashi, Kinnauri and Raji, each consists of three languages: Sanskrit (Indo-Aryan), Bhoti (Tibetan) and Kinnara. This third element is the basic structure of these languages. We know this third language as Kinnara. Thus Kinnara is a separate class of languages, different from the Tibeto-Burman and Indo-Aryan. A few vocabularies have been added to them from the other two languages. Kinnara is a class of languages and the others like Kanashi, Kinnauri, etc. are its branches. Thus Kanashi belongs to the Kinnara class of the Himalayan languages. This constitutes the basic structure of the language. It incorporates vocabulary from Tibetan and Sanskrit-Pahari languages. Thus Kanashi, Kinnauri, etc. belong to the class of the Himalayan languages of Kinnara.

**Tibetan connection of Kanashi:** It appears that the connection of Kanashi with Tibetan is very limited. One of the fundamental features of Tibetan language is that it takes adjective after the subject. But this feature is not found in the Kanashi. We give a few examples below:

| English | Tibetan | Kanashi |
|---|---|---|
| Long man. | mi (subject) ring-mo (adjective). | lamos (adjective) munukh (subject). |
| Small field. | zhing chhung-ngun. | phāk ṡo. |
| Big field. | zhing chhed-mo. | thek ṡo. |

Here we observe that in Kanashi the adjectives are placed before the subject unlike in Tibetan. Thus in this respect the two languages differ from each other. In vocabulary there are some words in Kanashi which are common with Tibetan. We give a few examples below:

| English | Kanashi | Tibetan |
|---|---|---|
| Fire | mi | me |
| Wood | shing | shing |
| Butter, ghee | mar | mar |
| Meat | sha | sha |
| Salt | chhat | sha |
| Eye | mig | mig |
| To die | shig | chhi-ba |

Tibetan association of Kanashi in vocabulary is clear. Here although the presence of Tibetan words in Kanashi is very small but this is very significant. The period of association of the two languages appears to belong to some early stage of development of the two languages.

We may have a rough assessment of the stages of development of Kanashsi in incorporating words from the two other languages. The adoption of some words from Tibetan appears to have occurred first. This could have happened at a very early stage when the population was still at the place of its origin. We have no knowledge of the words lent from Kanashi to Tibetan. No Tibetan word has been adopted at the present place of Malana. The Sanskrit-Pahari words appear to have been adopted in their interactions with the surrounding population at the present place of settlement. The same pattern of development is exhibited in the numerals. In Kanashi the first four figures of numerals are from its basic language Kinnara. The fifth is from Tibetan and the rest are from Sanskrit-Pahari.

The characteristics of a small link of Kanashi with Tibetan worked magically to keep Malana firmly footed to the soil of its origin, the Himalaya, otherwise stage was set to shift Malana to the plains of India or to some unknown country in the west including Alexander's birth place, (Tobdan, 2021b:170-177). .

We are aware that there lived Kinnaras at the headwaters of Chandrabhaga which is today known as Lahul. Kinnaras still live in Kinnaur close to Lahul. The habitation of the Kinnaras might have included Spiti and also the valley of the headwater of Satluj which is presently known as Guge. In the time of Ashoka it was known as Suvanna Bhumi and Hiuen Tsiang calls it Suvarnagotra. The inhabitants of this Kinnaraland, the ancient Kimpurushvarsha, spoke a language of their own. They are Kinnaras, the people who speak Kinnara language which has many dialects or branches. They originated in the Himalaya. Their culture however did not expand beyond the place of their birth. In the long course of its history it was compressed from both directions north and south and now there remain only a few samples. The examples are Malana, some sections of the society in Lahul, Kinnaur, and many small communities in Uttrakhand, and may be more. In Uttrakhand there are many small linguistic cultures who are designated as Bhotiya. From their ethnology and languages they may be Kinnaras. There may be some element of Tibetan in culture due to their regular interaction with their neighbours.

As regards the migration of Malanis we stick to our proposition we had made long back. Now we come with stronger evidences and with more confidence. The immigration of the population like those of Malanis may have started with the expansion of the Central Tibetan population towards the west after the establishment of Central Tibetan Empire. There could have been some other causes also and different times. This is also the view of Rahul. The Malanis and some others might have been pushed further.

To one such uprooted groups must belong the people of Malana who now live in a completely isolated village in Malana, (Tobdan, 1984: 35). They have been living protecting themselves i. e. their ethnicity, their culture specially the ancient system of their administration and their language. They might have been taught the administrative system sometime after coming of the Ashoka's missionaries who reached both at the heads of Chandrabhaga and the Satluj. Their original habitat might have been at the headwaters of Chandrabhaga or to the east somewhere upto the head of Satluj. Spiti is also a possible place which is found to have been completely changed in population.

Thus the people of Malana are Kinnaras who originated in the high Himalaya from where they migrated to the present place of settlement. Malana lives with things much of its original place with the same identity, but now changing fast.

# 6

# Kiratas: Inhabitants of the Eastern Part of the Himalaya

Kiratas [Kirāta] are considered among the early people of India. They are found mentioned earliest in the Sanskrit literature in the Vedas. S.K. Chatterji writes that, "The name Kirata is for the first time found in the Yajurveda in connection with the Purushamedha or Man-offering sacrifice, where list of all kinds of human beings and animals symbolically or figuratively offered to the gods as sacrifice is given. We find the following passage: 'A Kirata, for the caves, and Jambhaka (long-toothed man) for the slopes, a kimpurusa, an ugly man, a wild man, an ape, for the mountains. Then in the Atharvaveda we have a reference to Kirata girl who digs for a herbal. The young maid of Kirata race, a little damsel, digs the drugs. Digs it with shovels wrought of gold on the high ridges of the hills," (Chatterjee: 1974: 27).

From the method of description given by the ancient authors we can make a little guess about the position of habitation of the three kinds of people described here. The Kimpurushas lived in the mountains, at the highest level; Jambhak on the mountain slopes and the Kiratas lived in the plains or near the plains. Chatterji further writes that 'from the Yajurveda onwards the mountain regions of North and North-eastern India – the Himalayas particularly, are well attested as the abode of the Kiratas.' Chatterji notes that the Kiratas lived in the Himalayas, particularly in its northern and north-eastern part. Kiratas after the Vedas are found mentioned in the Epics, the Puranas and other literature. Kiratas were a Himalayan people.

In the Mahabharata in one of the acts of a story, 'Siva, assumes the form of a Kirata. He bears their characteristics of a huntsman. taking up a handsome bow and arrows resembling snakes of virulent poison. He quickly moves down from the high onto the middle of the Himalaya to meet Arjuna. The Lord comes with Uma and the swarm of the followers all in the garb of Kirata's, (Menon, Ramesh, 2009, Vol. 2: Kairat Parva). The epic has so much consideration for the Kiratas that a whole section is allotted for their description named as Kairata Parva in the Mahabharata.

Here the real Kiratas are not visible. But they have been portrayed with consideration. Some of their major characteristics are highlighted. It shows that the Kiratas were a people who lived on hunting mostly and they were warlike. The story, as noted by the commentators, is likewise reproduced in the plot of the poetical work of Bharvi in his Kiratarjuniyam.

Motichandra quoting Mahabharata writes, "Bhim conquered the Kiratas basing his operations from the Videha country or the modern Tirhut division of Bihar. A very interesting description of the Kiratas and their territories is given in the Upayanaparva. They are mentioned as living on the northern slopes of the Himalayas from where the sun rises, (Motichandra, 1945: 84). The territory of the Kiratas is shown here in the eastern part of the Himalaya.

Motichandra furnishes more information on the appearance and the economic system of the Kiratas from Mahabharata. He writes, "The Kiratas are represented as wearing skins, they lived on the tubers and fruits. The Ramayana represents as wearing thick top knots. The Kirata's presents to Yudhisthira fully represented the products of their country. They brought skins, precious stones and gold," (Motichandra, 1945: 85).

B.C. Law describes the Kiratas as, "Kiratas were a non-Aryan mountain tribe possessing a rude culture." Later he identifies them with the Kiratas of Nepal, (Law, B.C. 1943: 282). He writes that the Kiratas are referred to in the Mahabharata together with the Yaunas or Yavannas, Kambojas, Gandharas and Barbaras, who all dwelt in the northern region or Uttrapath, while the Ramayana mentions them alongwith the Mlecchas or barbarians, another non-Aryan tribe. Here are named the people contemporaneous and living in the neighbourhood of the Kiratas.

In the Ramayana, Chatterji writes, "The Pandava hero, son of Kunti, coming to the Vaideha, land close to Indra Mountains, defeated the seven Kirata rulers," (Chatterjee,1974: 30). Thus they had their own territories, had organised themselves into states and they themselves ruled those states.

"According to the Puranic cosmography," writes S.M. Ali, "Bharatavarsa was divided into nava khandas, or nine divisions or units. The ninth khanda extends for 1,000 yojanas. On the east live Kiratas, on its west, Yavanas," (Ali, 1966: 127). Here in the territorial division of the land the Kiratas are shown to live in the east. On the other end, in the west, live Yavanas. The Kiratas are described here as of golden colour. Chatterji writes, "The Kiratas hair done in pointed top-knots, pleasant to look upon, shining his gold, able to move under water, terrible, veritable tiger men, so are they famed."

These ancient treatises show the expanse of the presence of the Kiratas and their reputation as warriors. They lived in the forests by hunting. The Kiratas lived in the Himalayas, in the eastern part of it.

The Kiratas appear in the sacred literature continuously. They are also represented in the secular literature. Bana (1st half of VII th century C.E.) writes in his work Kadambari, that Chandrapid, the prince was on the campaign of winning the whole earth. "Then..., he once conquered and seized the city called Suvarnapura, which was not very far from the Eastern ocean, and was the residence of the Kiratas who dwell on the Hemakuta mountain and who prowled about in the vicinity of Mount Kailash," (Kale, 1924: 164). The author here says that Kiratas live in Hemakuta i.e. Kailash and not far from the eastern sea.

Kalhan's Rajatarangini has references to Kiratas in the manner that, "King Meghavahan saw a Kirata with head bent down and a Sabra ready to severe his head in order to sacrifice him to a Chandika in order to save his son. The king stopped the affair and offered himself for the offer upon the explanation of the cause of sacrifice by the Shabra." The Translator places king Meghvahana as the 28th in the geneology and to the period of C.E. 24-57. At another place, in the same work, it gives that, "By igniting forest fires, by constructing decoys and traps the Kiratas slay the lions and other animals, but themselves meet death through sudden landslides in the jungle," (Pandit, 1935: Tarang-III:39; VIII-358). The Kiratas appear here in their ancient social position. It is not known if Kiratas lived in Kashmir.

**Modern Studies**

B.C. Law places at one place the Kirata land in Tibet. B.S. Upadhyaya identifies the Kiratas of Kalidas with the Tibetans or Indo-Tibetans. He writes that, "The Kiratas of Kalidasa were positively the Tibetans of

Tibeto-Burmese of Ladakh, Zanskar and Rupshu. Yet their identification with the Tibetans living round the Mansarovar lake cannot be precluded as although they are encountered after and not before the Ganges which lay to the east of Karakuram pass. The Mansarovara lake lay in the same range. There is no doubt about the fact that even the people of Bhutan and its vicinity have been called Kiratas. But Kalidasa places them near about Ladakh," (Upadhyaya, 1947: 61- 62).

On the history of Ladakh about the period concerned, the historians like Petech, write that Ladakh was inhabited by a different kind of people, who are not related with the Kiratas. They were called Daradas and were well known to the Greek authors.

Hermanns and Chatterji identify in the vast existing population of the Himalaya with greatly varied cultural constituents, a prominent common element of Mongoloid feature, which in their view existed since ancient times. Hermanns, an eminent anthropologist, addresses them as Indo-Tibetans; Chatterji, an eminent Linguist, as Indo-Mongoloids and Grierson, an eminent Linguist, as Tibeto-Himalayan. Chatterji appears to take the phrase as a synonym to the ancient term Kirata and perhaps it also includes other similar tribes like the ancient Kinnaras, Nagas, etc. In their view some of the existing Himalayan tribes have a common feature of Mongloid character. This is a fact accepted and generally found mentioned in the works of the modern scholars on the subject. This is a fact indicated even in certain ancient works. The ancient term "Cīna" which refers to the people wholly Indian expresses the same fact. Some important aspects appear to be unknown here.

Regarding the advent of the particular culture Chatterji writes, "It was when the bases of the distinctive Hindu or Austric Dradividian-Aryan culture were being laid that another racial (or, rather, linguistic-cultural) group, the Mongoloid Sino-Tibetan, made its presence felt in the country," (Chatterji, 1974: 14). Regarding "The Mongoloid Element in Himalayan and North-Eastern India" and the arrival of the Mongoloid population Chatterji writes, "The history of the arrival into India of the various Mongoloid groups speaking dialects of the Sino-Tibetan speech family is not known, nor have all the various languages and dialects in the family been satisfactorily classified. It would appear that their presence in India was noted by the 10th century B.C. when the Veda books were compiled. The Composite Hindu (i.e., Austrict-Dravidian-Aryan, or Indo-Gangetic) civilization reached the Mongoloid peoples of Northern and North-Eastern mountains and plains from about that date," (Chatterji, 1974: 15-16).

On this point Hermanns writes, "The southern Himalayan mountains in Nepal, Sikkim and Bhutan, with their steep and narrow valleys and many tracts of land offer favourable retreat for racial remnants what surprised us most about these various groups of peoples was the medley of Mongloids and non-Mongoloids. Both these groups stand in deep contrast to those Aryans who immigrated from India. According to tradition Kirata are the oldest inhabitants of Nepal. They were also called Kiranti or Kichak. These names were originally used for the Khambu or Rai who are also called Jimdar," (Hermanns, 1954: 1 & 7). Modern scholars also employ the terms Bhot and Bhotiya from the folk tradition for the people living in the regions of high Himalaya nearer to the Tibetan borders. The two scholars appear in their studies comprehensive.

Other scholars present different views on the subject. Singh, G.P. states that, 'Kirata once constituted the largest tribal group in ancient India extending from the pre-Vedic age down to the 12th century A.D. Those, who had been living in caves, mountain and forest regions of, particularly, Northern and Eastern Himalayan regions ever since the Prehistoric Age, and known as the Adivasis, aboriginals, were called for the first time as Kirata by the later Vedic Aryans. They belonged not only to the non-Aryan social groups as, hitherto, believed by many, but to the Aryan as well. They were, by and large of indigenous origin. Their racial ethnology differed from region to region. The geographical distribution of the Kiratas, as a whole does not warrant the assumption that all of them came from east of China, Tibet and Burma and were Mongoloids. Actually they were of mixed origin. After getting all the available evidences thoroughly examined, we can easily conclude that there was no migration of the Kirata population from outside India before the beginning of the Christian era,' (Singh, 1990:449-451).

Scholars describe Kiratas as non-Aryan, pre-Aryan and as the aboriginal Indians. Some scholars write them as degraded class. Lexicons often explain Kirata also as Malechha or Nishad.

## Kiratas: The Inhabitants of Eastern Part of the Himalaya

Himalaya geographically in modern times is divided into three divisions: Western, Central and Eastern. In the earlier literature Himalaya is found divided into two parts. We generally read only eastern Himalaya. The ancient literature generally describe, as we have seen above, the Kiratas inhabiting the eastern part of the Himalay, i.e. the eastern half of the Himalaya.

Shukla writes that according to the Ramayana, the Kiratas have been included among the aboriginal tribes. Further, 'Kirata land is called Kirata-dvipa, which lay in the east of the Himalaya, and was inhabited by the Kiratas – a non-Aryan mountain tribe possessing a rude culture. At present they are known as Kirati or Kiranti residing in the valley of Dudkosi and the Karki rivers of Nepal along the south-eastern slopes of the Himalayas,' (Shukla, R.K., 2003:264).

Matsya Purana places the Kiratas in the east and the Yavanas in the west of India, as we have seen above. Agrawala, V.S., places the Kiratas of the above source in Madhyadesh and explains the Kiratas as 'the people settled along the foot-hills of the Himalayas.' Dowson writes as: "Foresters and mountaineers living in the mountains east of Hindustan.' 'There is a tribe in the Central Himalayas called Kirantis.' From all these sources we arrive at a conclusion that Kiratas are Himalayan people and they lived in the central Himalaya or eastern part of the Himalaya.

**Occupation**

According to Kalidasa (4th-5th century C.E.) in his work Raghuvansham, Raghu, the king on the campaign of universal victory, from the west moves into the Himalaya towards the east. He meets there Kiratas, Utsavaketu and Kinnaras. Kiratas "could learn the heights of Raghu's elephants by the height of the marks made on the bark of deodar tree by the ropes with which they were tied to them," (Chakladar, 1925: 23). Thus the Kiratas lived in the Himalaya mountains. Kiratas possessed so thorough knowledge about the behaviours of the elephants that they could judge the heights of the elephants from the marks of ropes left on the trunks of the deodar trees with which they were tied. There were forests wherein also there lived elephants. This could be in the lower Himalaya. The Kiratas were well acquainted with the behaviours of the domesticated elephants. They might have been employing them economically. They had made a great stride in economic development.

Kiratas were famed warriors. There are several references showing that the Kiratas were employed as army and they were fine warriors. B.C.

Law writes that, "In the Mahabharata ranged on Duryodhana's side in the Kurukshetra war are Sivis, Kiratas, etc. (B.C. Law 1943: 84). We saw that in the Mahabharata Siva Mahadeva taking the guise of Kirata, appeared as a Senapati, leading the army of his men also in the garb of Kiratas.

Hunting as we have seen in the Mahabharata above, was one of the popular occupations of the Kiratas. In the ancient Indian architecture of a king's palace, according to Shukla, a section was constructed for the use of the hunters which was named 'Kirātālaya' = "Chamber for hunters," (Shukla, L.K., 1972:113). Literally it means 'a house for use of the Kirātas,' but practically it meant a section built for the use of the hunters of the king. From this we understand that the term was derived from the profession that was principally followed by the Kiratas. This is an evidence unchallengingly proving that the Kiratas are a historical people and hunting is their principle profession. Chakladar writes that, "The Kiratas are mentioned by Kalidasa as a hunting tribe going in pursuit of deer and other animals." This important qualification of the Kiratas made them uncontestingly eligible as armies of the kings. They were fit to fight everywhere, on the land and in the sea, as we find references.

The profession of hunting and rearing elephants made them a home trained excellent warrior. They were good drivers of elephants and sitting over the elephants they could use bow and arrows most skilfully. This made them fine warring armies of the Rajas in the ancient times. They earned a distinctive name. They might have formed the large section of the armed strength of the ancient Rajas.

**Kiratas in Uttrakhand**

About the situation of the Kiratas in Garhwal and Kumaon, the Gazetteer of Garhwal informs that, "Vishnu Purana, the Mahabharata, and the Varahamihira mention a number of tribes dwelling on the borders of Bharat and of these the Sakas, the Nagas, the Khasas, the Hunas and the Kirates are to be connected with the Kumaon Himalayan region. The last named may be dismissed with the briefest notice for whatever their early importance, they have now disappeared entirely from Garwal, though they are doubtfully identified with the Rajis, a rapidly dwindling tribe of foresters living in Askot of eastern Kumaon," (Walton: 1910:111). It thus enumerates that Kiratas, alongwith other well known ancient tribes, lived in Garhwal.

The Gazetteer of Almora writes that "The Kiratas or Rajya Kiratas were a tribe of foresters, and they are doubtfully identified with the Rajis – an almost extinct race found in Askot. These represent themselves as descendants of one of aboriginal princes of Kumaon. "who fled with his family to escape the destruction thrown up by an usurper, and in virtue of their regal descent they never salute any one," (Walton: 1911: 162-163). They are an ancient people, it is a valuable fact. These note that Kiratas formed one of the inhabitants of the region but now they have disappeared.

Pati Ram gives description about the appearance of the Kiratas in Garhwal, that, "After the Kurukshetra war some of the old Aryan clans became extinct and new tribes came into prominence so that at the end of Epic period or in the Buddhist age, we find Garhwal inhabited in the north by Kiratas and Tanganas. Ptolemy writes that these tribes were populated from the Jamuna to the Sarda (Kalinadi in Kumaon) and the whole country was called Tangunoi," (Pati Ram, 1916: 12).

Atkinson enumerates some existing tribes who live in isolation and have ancient origin in Uttrakhand comprising Garhwal and Kumaon. He writes, "To the north in the inter alpine valleys of Bhot we have a decided Tibetan origin and shows affinities are found in the trans-Himalayan tribes of Hundes. They are Known as Bhotiyas by the people of the lower hills who in turn as are designated Khasiyas by the Bhotiyas, whilst the people of the adjoining portion of Tibet are known as Hunas or Huniyas. In addition to the tribes already enumerated there are Rajis or Rajyas the modern representations of Rajya-Kiratas and the Tharus and Bhoksas of the Tarai lowlands and traces of the Nagas and Sakas, whilst others contend, (Atkinson, 1981, II-I: 270). The modern scholars agree that there lived Kiratas in Uttrakhand region.

Dabral writes that the Kiratas belonged to Mongol race. He equates them with Keer and also writes Kilata for Kirata. He further writes that, "Kinnara and Kirata were two branches of Mongol Race who spread on the slopes of the Himalaya from east to west. It is assumed that Kiratas came after the Kinnaras and were pushed forth towards the west. In the time of Kalidas the Kinnara and Kiratas both lived side by side in the valley of Ganga," (Dabral, 1995: 497). Dabral also has some other explanations, all varying, about the Kiratas in Uttrakhand.

## Kiratas in Buddhist Literature

References about the Kiratas found in the Buddhist literature are rare. But the following two from the Buddhist literature are the rarest and the most valuable among the whole literature available about the Kiratas.

Asvaghosh (c. C.E. 1st-2nd century) refers in his work Buddhacaritam that when Siddhartha, the historical Buddha in youth, went for a round of the capital city of Kapilvastu, there stood many kinds of people on the road side to greet the prince and watch the royal procession. Among them were a group of Kiratas and all bowed down to the god in the procession, (Asvaghosa: Buddhacarita, 3/12). Kiratas, thus, did not live far away from Kapilvastu, in the eastern part of the Himalaya. They appear till recent times living close around the same area.

As already observed above, an inscription was discovered from the ruins of a monastery at the famous Buddhist site at Nagarjunikonda. It refers to the instance of sending the missionaries in c. 250 B.C.E. to different countries including the Himalayas. The inscription belongs to c. C.E. 250.

It records that the team of the theras headed by Majhhima brought the people of the Himalaya into the refuge of the Three Jewels. The people of the Himalaya is named here in two parts as Cīna and Kirāta. The people of the eastern half of the Himalaya are named as Kirata. Thus the inscription in the third century C.E. shows that the people living on the eastern half of the Himalaya were undoubtedly addressed as Kirata.

Rahul confirms the same important historical fact. He writes that, "at one time the country of the Kinnaras in the Himalaya extended from the headwaters of Ganga to the west upto the headwaters of Satluj and Chandrabhaga. The Kiratas lived from the headwaters of Ganga upto Nepal," (Rahul, 1953: 42).

We observe Greek scholars referring to Kiratas in India. McCrindle writes that Nonnos, a Greek scholar, writes c. beginning of the 5th or 6th century C.E. that, "Near them (Kings and women) were ranged the Cirradioi used to naval warfare, but in boats, of skins, their chiefs were Thyamis and Olkaros, sons of Tharseros, the rower," (McCrindle: 1901: 199). McCrindle explains in the note that by the Cirradioiis meant the Kirata, a race spread along the spheres of Bengal to eastward of the mouth of Ganges as far as Arracan. This shows the eastern limit of habitations of the Kiratas and it also shows that they were also skilled in the naval warfare. They are described by the author of another Greek work who calls them Kirrhadai as savage with flat noses. He places them on the east to the west of the Ganges. Ptolemy describes the Kirata as Airrhadioi.

Alberuni (c. C.E. 1030) writes that the river Ganges which is the middle and main stream flows through the regions of Gandharva, the musicians, Kimnara, Yakshas, Rakshasa, Vidyadhara, Uraga, i.e. those who creep on their breast, the serpents, Kalapagrama, i.e. the city of the most virtuous Kimpurusha, Khasa, the mountaineers, Kirata, Pulinda, the hunters in the plains. ....Of the eastern Ganges arms, the Hradini flows through the countries among others Kirata. Alberuni here is describing about the inhabitants of the middle of the Himalaya. Alberuni describes the Kiratas twice once in the middle division of the Himalaya but near the plains as neighbours of the Pulindas. Secondly he describes them in the east along the river Hridini, a tributary of the Ganges. This whole region consisted their habitat.

**Kiratas in Nepal:** Scholars in the modern times have located the Kiratas inhabiting the eastern part of Nepal. The region of habitation of the Kiratas agrees with the descriptions made by the ancient scholars. The area of their habitat got contracted very much during the course of long history.

Regmi, a historian from Nepal, writes regarding the valley of Kathmandu, that, "It is admitted by all that the Kiratas were the sole occupants of the valley for a long time from the earliest time recorded in history," (Regmi, 1952:1). He further writes that according to Nepalese tradition they occupied the Kathmandu valley before the Licchvi dynasty just prior to and during the years of Christian era. Nowadays going by this name they live in the eastern parts of Nepal: the Rais, Limbu and Yakhas.

Hermanns writes that, "According to tradition kirata are the oldest inhabitants of Nepal. They were also called Kiranti or Kichak. These names were originally used for the Khambu or Rai who are also called Jimdar," (Hermanns, 1954: 7). Mitra says that,"Kirata and Kiranti are the same. Earliest reference to them is found in the Puranas. ... The Kiratis, it is said, occupied the country to the east of 'Bharata,' and in the list of peoples further on we find them alongwith the 'Barbaras,' and are told in the note that these latter are considered by all the authorities as borderers and foreigners and nations not Hindu. The Kirantis are still numerous in

Dinajpur which was the part of ancient Matsyades, all the inhabitants of which were considered as foreigners and borders. They are as Limbus an important segment of the population of Sikkim and as Kirantis of Nepal," (Mitra, 1953: 222). Risley explains Kiranti and specifies their country as. "A native of the Kirat-des or mountainous country lying between the Dudd-Kosi and the Karki rivers in Nepal. The term includes the Kambu, Limbu, and Yakha tribes, and the Danuar, Hayu and Thams also claim to be Kiranti," (Risley, 189I: 490). "The Kiratas, or Kichaks, have been already mentioned as occupying the country east from Nepal Proper. They seem always to have been a warlike and enterprising people," writes Hamilton.

We here get a glimpse of Nepal's longer past. Daniel Wright gives a legend saying that, "The Kiratis came into Nepal at the 15,000th year of Dwapar yuga and they ruled over the country for 10,000 years. The gods came into the country after the Kiratis." This indicates that the Kiratas were the original inhabitants of Nepal. Then they appear again as a conqueror. In the time of the Raja Bhuvana Sinha, of cowherd dynasty, the Kiratis came from the east and conquered the kingdom. Yalambar was their first raja who ruled for 13 years", (Wright, 1877: 109). They ruled for 29 generations.

Daniel Wright provides complete list of all the 29 rulers which are also found in the work of Sylvan Levi. Levi has worked on the history of Kiratas in Nepal in much detail. Daniel further writes that these Kirata Rajas lived in an inaccessible Darbar built in the jungles of Gokarna. During the reign of the 14th Raja Sthunko Asokaraja visited Nepal. "In the reign of this Raja, the Raja of Pataliputra (Patna), having heard the fame of Nepal as a sacred place and having obtained the permission of his spiritual guide, Upagupta Bhikshu, came on a pilgrimage to Nepal, accompanied by his family, and followed by a large number of his subjects. He visited every holy place, and bathed in every sacred water and went to Swayambhu, Guhjeswari, and eight Buddha Bitaragas or chaityas. He also built several chaityas. His daughter Charumati, while playing one day saw an iron arrowhead, turned into stone by god, and determined to remain in Nepal, having concluded from this that it was a land of miracles wrought by the gods. The Raja therefore, gave her in marriage to a descendant of Chhetri, named Devapala, gave them 3,600 ropanis of land and everything else requisite, and then returned to his own country." It is further stated that Charumati later on also built a Vihar.

The names of the Rulers are in a different language. They don't match with the form of languages of the class of Indo-Aryan or Tibeto-Himalyan. Then the Kirata rulers were expelled by the Somavansis. According to Sylvan Levi "the dynasty of the Kiratas number 26 or 29, and they ruled for a period between 1118 and 1581 years".

Kirckpatrick writes on the subject that, "This dynasty, however, was put an end to, in the person of Bhowany Singh, by Yellung, Kerraut, who invaded and conquered Nepaul with an army of Kerrauts, a tribe then occupying the country stretching from the Dhoodh-Kousi to the confines of Dewah Durmah, and, the remains of which are now scattered over the mountainous tract lying between that river and eastern extremity of the valley of Nepaul. The reign of Yellung, it is pretended, lasted 90 years and 3 months." The Kiratas (Kerrauts) were disposed of their kingdom by Nevesit, a Chhetri of the Soorajbansi race, (Kirkpatrick,1811: 257-259). His successors were Duskham, Bullacha, etc. There are 27 kings named here, who ruled for 1581 years rather 1630. The author corrects it to its half.

In the 18th century C.E. there lived people known as Kirata occupying an independent territory. Father Giusepee, a Christian missionary, arrived in Nepal in the beginning of 1769, (Giusepee, 1807:307-322). He writes that among the three principal cities viz., Kathmandu, Lalit Pattan, and, "the third principal city to the east of Lalit Pattan is called Bhatgan, contains about 12,000 families extends towards the east to the distance of five or six days journey, and borders upon another nation, also Independent, called Kiratas (Ciratas), who profess no religion." "The king of Gorkha (Gorcha) having thus in the space of four years made himself master also of the country of Kiratas (Ciratas) to the east of it and of other kingdoms, as far as the border of Cooch Bihar."

Giusepee writes that the Kiratas did not practice any religion. This is a strong sign of their being ancient people. Such groups of primitive people have unbalanced cultural developments, just as here they have weak religion. At other places some other aspect of the culture is missing. Some other tribes don't have word for greeting nor do they have such custom of saluting. But their knowledge in respect of certain cases like the names and uses of the wild plants, minute and detailed expressions in respect of some grammatical parts in their languages, etc. surpass those of any developed cultures. These Kirata people are ancient people. The Kiratas of Nepal are the same as found mentioned in the ancient literature of India.

Thus we observe that the Kiratas were an ancient historical people who are named with other tribes in the ancient works. They lived in the Himalayas, in the eastern part of the Himalaya. They were seen living around the same area since the early till the recent times.

Kiratas and Kinnaras both were inhabitants of the Himalaya. Both were aboriginals. The two may be differentiated from the facts that the Kinnaras lived in the higher Himalaya, Kiratas lived in the mountains but nearer to the plains; Kinnaras were inhabitants of the Western Himalaya, Kiratas were inhabitants of the eastern Himalaya. The geography of the Himalaya is such that while the western part of it stretches long the eastern part rises slowly from the plains to the heights.

# 7

# The Kīras of Kashmir

References to a people called Kīra (also known as Kīraka) are found in the history of some parts of India, the northern and middle. The references generally quote the term in brief as Kīra but having little further detail about it. It may be found mostly used in contempt. They are often depicted as fighting or invading troops. The term is not used by the people themselves but by others as a reference. In the history of Kashmir and Himachal Pradesh they are sometimes presumed to be Tibetan or Yarkandi invaders. In an inscription from Central India they are told to have actually come into contact with Bhotas, Tibetans. The term is somewhat obscure and the people remain unidentified properly.

In Himachal Pradeh the Kīras attacked on Bharmaur (the old state of Brahmapura) in Chamba and killed the king. At Baijnath in Kangra they had a settlement called Kīragrāma. The authors of the 'History of the Panjab Hill States' write that, "They (Kīras) also held Baijnath in the Kangra valley which was anciently called Kīragrāma," (Hutchison & Vogel, 1933-I: 281). Although Kīras are quite famed in name yet they themselves remain obscure and a people little known.

**Kīras in the History of Himachal Pradesh:** The Vansavali of Chamba state records that Bharmaur was once invaded by the Kīras in the reign of Lakshmi Varman. Hutchison & Vogel write that, "Lakshmi Varman (800) has not been long in power when the country was visited by an epidemic of a virulent and fatal character, resembling cholera or plague. Large number fell victims to the disease and the State was in a measure depopulated. Taking advantage of the desolation which prevailed, a people, bearing the name of 'Kīra' in the Chronicle, invaded Brahmapura and having killed the Raja, took possession of the territory. It is uncertain who the Kīras were," (Hutchison & Vogel, 1933-I: 281).

The narration in the Vansavali goes on to say that, the queen, who was pregnant was rescued by the ministers, together with the family-priest. Then they brought her to a country ruled by Prabhoga. There they stayed many years with the guru of the king. Once the guru seeing marks of royalty in the child asked his mother about their background. The attendants revealed the truth. Then the guru took him to the town of Sukhet and presented him to the king. The king kept both child and the mother with honour. The boy was named Musan-varman, so named because he was protected by the mice at the time of his birth on the way. When he came of age the king Prabhoga gave him his own daughter in marriage with the village of Pāngī and great wealth and gave him also a huge army. Then that Musana-varman came hastily and slew all Kīrakas and settled as ruler in his own country, (Vogel, 1911: 92). Thus the Kīras remained here for some time and then they were expelled. That the Kīras settled here is evidenced from some cultural traditions still available from the district.

Related to the Kīras we quote another old tradition current in the history of Chamba. A record of the Punjab government mentions Rana Jodhbir Singh, Ulansa, among the Cheifs of Chamba state, as the head of the oldest jagirdar family in the state of Chamba as: "His ancestor is said to have come from Kulu alongwith Raja Mushan Varma (820), and to have assisted that Raja in his reconquest of the territory from the Kīra invaders and for these and subsequent services he received a jagir at Ulansa. Many members of his family have rendered military services in past times, and the head of the family in 1794 was killed at Nerti [in Kangra] with Raja Raj Singh," (Punjab Govt., 1918: 17).

The state named Sukhet, where the queen of Chamba had taken refuge upon the Kīra invasion, as referred above in the Vansavali of Chamba, is identified with Suket, the ancient state adjacent to Mandi, now forming part of district Mandi. The piece of information contained in the Vansavali about Sukhet is fully incorporated in the history of Suket. The Gazetteer gives another instance related to Kīra in Suket. "An interesting tradition exists in the Rana family of Kanihara near Dharmsala, which claims descent from Suket. It is said that the Duthain, or the second son of the Suket Raja, possibly Bir Sen, was sent in command of the army and acted as Regent of Brahmaur. At a later time the family removed to Kanihara then in Chamba territory," (Beotra, 1924: 12, Note-2).

Chamba is considered as one of the oldest states in India and is rich in the matter of historical records in the form of inscriptions on copper-plate grants ranging for long period in addition to the Vansavali. One of such inscriptions contains a record, which is more specific, referring to an invasion by the enemy forces led by the Kīras. The inscription was first translated by Kielhorn (1888:7-13) and then was re-edited and re-translated by Vogel. The valuable document yielded the definite date which helped the historians of the state to assign reliable dates to the Rajas of Chamba contained in the genealogical list in the Vansavali.

The inscription belongs to the period of Asatavarman (1080-1105) and refers to Sahillavarman's (c. 920-40) victory over the stormy attack of the combined forces of Kīras, Dogras and Saumatikas. From the language of the document the attack appears to have been very powerful. It reads that Sahilla, "was a fresh rain cloud to extinguish in a moment the mighty blazing fire of the Kīra forces, fanned, as by the wind, by the Lord of Durgara, assisted by the Saumatikas, whose camp was manifestly crushed by the fearful frown produced on the slope of his (Sahilla's) forehead. Sahilla's alliance was humbly sought by the ruler of Trigarta," (Vogel, 1911: 194-95). Thus the Kīras had been active in the history of Chamba for some period.

**Kīragrāma (Baijnath) – A Kīra Settlement:** At Baijnath, about fifty kilometers north of Kangra, there is an ancient temple dedicated to Shiva Vaidyanath. In the temple there are two large inscriptions called Prasastis, eulogies, which give good information about the occasion of construction of the temple. Besides these, there are two other small inscriptions, one on the back of the large Nandi image outside the temple and the other on a pillar in the Mandapa, just on the right side as one enters the temple. On its outer wall there is another inscription placed during some repair work collected from a nearby lost Jaina temple.

The two inscriptions were translated by Buhler (Buhler, 1892: 97-118). Both these Prasastis were engraved in the same year. Buhler initially read the date of the inscription as Saka samvata 726, equivalent to C.E. 804. The reading of this date was re-examined by other scholars later on and now the date of writing of the inscriptions has been finally settled as Saka 1126 corresponding to C.E. 1204, (Vogel, 1909: 19-20).

The Prasasti provides that the village of Kīragrāma situated on the bank of river Binwa (Kandukabinduka), a tributary of Beas, is situated in the state of Trigarta. That village is ruled and protected by the strong armed Rana (Rajanaka) Lakshmana, also Lakshmanachandra. Evidently the village was then inhabited by the people named Kīra, from which it derived the name Kīragrāma, as also proposed by Vogel above.

**History of the lineage of Rana Lakshmana:** We gather from the Prasastis that the father of Rana Lakshmana, ruler of Kīrgrāma, was married to Lakshnika, daughter of his liege-lord, the king of Trigarta. Kanda, who was a Rajanaka, founded the family here eight generations before that of the present. Kanda was a great warrior. The inscription records list of all the generations with addition of some description about some of them. We give it below in brief.

Rajanaka Kanda, root of the precious clan, founded the dynasty. 'He was a destroyer of his foes, a conqueror of town, an untamable Skanda.' His son was Buddha. His son Vigraha 'caused the separation of the wives of his enemies from their beloved ones'. His son was Brahman, who 'possessed power to punish his enemies.'

His son Dombaka reflected his father's nature, 'who together with other princes took many villages.' His son Bhuvana 'made the forest the home of his proud foes, whose lion roar dreadful in battle.' Son Kalhana, 'passed over the heads of brave warriors.'

His son Bilhana possessed great power of mind and was terrible on account of his strength. He was married to Lakshanika, daughter of Hridayachandra, the king of Trigarta. He had two sons, named Rama and Lakshmana, the present Rana. Lakshmana ruled over the whole territory which Kanda possessed and the other feudatories of the kings of Trigarta ruled, (II, 10 to 21).

Buhler presumes that the area ruled by Lakshmana might have been larger than the single town. He writes that, "they probably possessed larger than a single village or small town," (Buhler, 1892: 102). In this respect the Prasasti gives clear description of the territory of the Rana in the words that, "there is in Trigarta the pleasant village of Kīrgrāma....protected by the strong-armed Rajanaka Lakshmana," (verse II, 10). That his territory comprised the only village or town Kīrgrāma is mentioned again` in verse II, 22. This is the territory Kanda founded and all the feudatories upto Lakshmana have been ruling over it. They could not extend their territory because Kīrgrāma, their state, lay within the territory of their liege-lord, Trigarta. They had not won the territory by conquering in battle. They were settled here with the courtesy and consent of the Raja of Trigarta. The inscription mentions that they are and always had been faithful to Trigarta. They founded the village of Kīrgrāma inhabited by Kīra people. Kanda was bestowed with the title and function of Rajanaka over Kīrgrāma.

Lakshmana, the present ruler, was a great warrior. He protected his subjects and the territory of Kīrgrāma with strong arms. In wars 'he was expert in wielding the sword' and was 'an invincible warrior.'

Now whereas he was hero in the battle fields, he was notorious in his town for his deplorable vices against the women of his town. But the Rana is now a changed man. He has realized that he is submerged in the deep well of delusion and that, 'I am only running after folly.' His vice against women, the wives of the others of the town, are explained in three verses, (I, 24-26).

One can guess the severity and extent of the kind of offence. In the first Prasasti, of 39 verses full half, unusual in proportion, is devoted for invocations addressed to Isvara, Gauri and Ganesh. Gauri is entreated more earnestly for grant of mercy for the great sin he confesses to have committed against women. The prayer goes much further in description than mere confession.

For the removal of his past sins he performed pilgrimage to Kedarnath in Garhwal, Uttrakhand, and made a vow, "henceforth shall all wives of others be sisters for me." This vow he maintained most earnestly and is described in poetical language: "Fresh youth, beautiful shape, liberality, sovereignty over a town, many flatterers, all these are his; if nevertheless his heart avoids the wives of others, what austerity is difficult to perform after that?" (I,25).

Regarding the construction of the temple there is no hint to indicate any specific contribution or even any kind of initiation in the work, worthy on the part of the Rana. He, however, allots as a contribution from the resources of the state for meeting the running expenses of the temple. The temple was built by the two merchant brothers, according to the inscription, "By him (Ahuk), a bee in the park of devotion, and by his brother (Manyuk) has been erected this temple of the slayer of Tripura," (I,29).

The temple was built to house an ancient Linga which was lying in open. Nayaka from Susarmana town, the head, and Thodhuka were the architect-masons. The Prasastis were composed by Rama, the prince of poets, whose father was a high official in the court of the king of Kashmir. The inscriptions were written after the completion of the construction, writes Buhler. These were engraved by Guhaka.

In due course the town of Kīragrāma adopted more respectable name Baijnath after the name of the temple and the Kīras, the common population, lost their distinctiveness. Other transformations occurring in the names of the surrounding towns may be Pralamba = Palampur; Navagrama = Nagrota; and some other. Nearby there is another temple, similar but slightly smaller, named Siddhesvara. The inscription in the temple was lost with the time. Since the name of the temple is the same as the name of the father of the two financers of the temple Ahuk and Manyuk, it probably was also built by the same two brothers in honour of their father Siddha.

A Jain temple was erected in Kīrgrāma in vikramasamvata 1296 equivalent to C.E. 1240, (Buhler, 1892). We gather from this that the town was still known by the same name as Kīrgrāma.

Kanda was Rajanaka and his ninth generation also holds the same position. Buhler writes emphatically that, "It shows that the Rajanakas of Kīrgrāma were noble Rajputs, and, though only feudal barons, stood high enough in the estimation of the world to be thought worthy of an alliance with the royal house of Jalandhara-Trigarta." This was a great step towards social development of this group of the class of Kīras. This status, however, they had attained already in Kashmir.

Looking at the list of the Rajanakas as seen above and reckoning the period of their history, it may be estimated that they had settled here in about tenth century. The period coincides with the war by Sahillavarman of Chamba with the Kīras, from which it may be presumed that it is the same group who fought on the side of Durgara. As they are suzerain to Trigarta they might have been prompted by Trigarta to settle here in exchange for services as armed force of the state.

Another fact noteworthy here is that Rana Lakshmana admits of having been of unchaste character which might have been curbed with the benevolent advice of his mother, the noble lady, the princess, daughter of the Raja of Trigarta. The society of the class of Kīra has earned a mark of distinctiveness in the eyes of the world throughout their history for harbouring different kinds of unusual habits and engaging in activities like harmful to the society.

**Kīras – Tibetan or Yarkandis:** Presence of the Kīras in Chamba and Baijnath was explained by some scholars as invasions by the Tibetans on suggestions from A.H. Francke, a scholar on the subject. Vogel explains the aspect in full: "To explain the existence of Tibetan princes in the valley of Brahmapura in early times, first of all the Vansavali (verse 48) of Chamba speaks of the conquest of Brahmor by Kīras, during the reign of Laksmivarman, one of the early historical rulers of the country. I feel much inclined to identify the Kīras with the Tibetans whose kings were often designated by the word Khri, throne. There was a dynasty of Khri Gyal, later Khri Sultans, in the Suru valley, (Ladakh). There were whole dynasties of Khris among the ancient Tibetan kings, and some of the greatest Tibetan conquerors, Khri-srong bde-btsan, Khri-lde gtsug-mes ag-tshoms, and Khri-tsong lde-btsan, have the word Khri in their names. This word is pronounced Khri, not Thi by the nearest Tibetan neighbours of Chamba and Kashmir, the people of Suru and Purig," (Vogel, 1911: 254-255).

Goetz at first disagrees with the above suggestion from Vogel. But he appears to arrive at the same conclusion when he writes, "The Kīra invasion which gave the coup de grace to the Brahmapura kingdom, can be identified with certainty. The term Kīra generally was used for the hardly known tribes in the hinterland of Kashmir, in the middle ages, when the Dards, Bhauttas, etc. were already known it referred mainly to those Tibetans who were not the immediate neighbours of the Himalayan Indians," (Goetz, 1955: 26-27). Some scholars appear to hold the same view still. But there is no historical example to suggest such a view.

One of the leading points forwarded to uphold this argument is the similarity of the term Kīra with the Tibetan word Khri. There is otherwise no reason to suggest such an improbable proposition. In Tibetan the word Khri, as suggested above, means throne and this epithet is assigned to some Tibetan monarchs in early period, whose names have all been referred to in full above. Any incursion from Tibetan borders so deep into the interiors of Himachal reaching the other end of it seems geographically impossible and would have been grossly an unwise decision. There appears nothing special to attract invaders from so far off.

### Kīras in Kashmir

In Kalhan's Rajatarangini a reference is made at one place to a people designated as Kīra as, "Also Jayacandra and other Kasmirians (and) Kīras, sent by Rajavardana, came to the side of the prince," (Stein-II,1900: VIII-2767), which belongs to the first half of twelfth century. Kīras here are seen as a fighting force within Kashmir in alliance with the Kashmirians in a war against the rebels of the kingdom and foreign forces.

Stein explains the term Kīra in the note that Kīra appears in the ethnographic list of Varahmihira's Brhatsamhita as the name of a race located in the NE along with Kasmirians, Abhisaras and Darads. He rejects the view as given by some scholars who say that, "Kīras represent as another designation of the inhabitants of Kashmir." Thus the Kīras in the view of Stein belong to Kashmir but they are different from the mainstream Kashmirians. He in support of his argument quotes another example. He writes that the name Kīra was actually borne by some people or tribe in the vicinity of Kashmir is shown by the Chamba copper-plate grant of Asata which mentions a victory of Sahilladeva, Raja of Chamba, over the Kīras, who are named there between the Durgaras, i.e. Dogras, and the Trigartas. It is curious that no other reference to the Kīras is found in Kashmirian texts, (Stein-II, 1900: VIII-2767, Note).

Vogel clarifies the various states involved in the war as found described in the Chamba copper-plate grant of Asata. He writes that Sahillavarman was in alliance with the Rajas of Kangra (Trigarta) and Kulu (Kuluta), and repulsed the combined attack of the Saumatikas and the Kīra troops of the Raja of Dugar i.e. Dogra (Durgara). The Saumatikas are undoubtedly the people of Sumarta a tract in the former Hill State of Basohli, or Balor [near Jammu, now in J&K], which is frequently mentioned in the Rajatarangini under the name of Vallapura." Vogel also writes, "Apparently the name Kīra occurs in Kīragrāma, the modern Baijnath in Kangra," (Vogel, 1911: 98-99). He further writes that the Kīras are also mentioned among other non-Aryan tribes in the Khajuraho inscription of Yasovarman Candella and others. Vogel now considers the Kīras as the people from Kashmir but, notably, are a non-Aryan race. It is now affirmed that the Kīras are natives of Kashmir.

**Kīra – Etymology:** It may be noted that in every reference found in its long and wide history and also current in usage at some places in Himachal the term is always written and pronounced as Kīra. We find no other variant of the term. The term is explained by various scholars but literal meaning of the word is not found. The term is not found used by the people themselves, perhaps a taboo for them, but used by the observers as a term of reference.

Lexicons, both Hindi and Sanskrit, in general explain the term Kīra as a name of the country of Kashmir and as the name of a people belonging to Kashmir, but no literal meaning of the term is given.

**The People called Kṛtyakāh**: Again in the Rajatarangini at an early period in the history of Kashmir in the time of Jalauk, third century BCE, there is description of a class of people named Kṛtyakāh resembling by name and corresponding in social status with the Kīras. Stein translates the relevant verse as, "We witches (kṛtyakāh) being by the side of Mount Lokāloka belong to the darkness (sin),' (verse I,137). The word kṛtyā comes again twice in the verses 146 and 147 in the same Tarang. Here the people are shown as belonging to Kashmir but geographically and as a social class they appear different. They are shown living in a remote area and are followers of the Buddha. There run a few verses describing the nature of their society and the faith they pursue. Once the king Jalauka was going to the temple of Vijyesvara. He met a woman in the way who asked him for some food. When he promised her whatever food she wanted she should ask, she changed her form and expressed her desire for human flesh. The king having renounced to kill, permitted her to take off what she liked from his own body.

The woman then said, "O king you must be a Bodhisattva, whose observance of vows is supported by absolute goodness (sattva)." The king being worshipper of the Siva did not know the Buddhas. He asked, "who is the Bodhisattva for whom you know me?"

She spoke to the king, "I have been sent forth by the Baudhas whom in your anger you have injured." "We witches (Kṛtyakāh) living by the side of Mount Lokāloka belong to the darkness. Putting our whole trust in the Bodhisattvas we long for liberation from the darkness. ... There was a monastery belonging to us in which the beating of drums once disturbed your sleep, and incited by the advice of wicked men you have destroyed the monastery. The angry Buddhists sent me."

After she had made the king promise to build a Vihara the divine sorceress (kṛityā) disappeared with eyes beaming with joy. Thereupon the king built the Kṛtyāśrama Vihār, (Stein-I, 1900: I- 131-147)

The primary form of the term employed by Kalhan and other scholars in their various versions of Rajatarangini here is kṛtya or kṛtyā. Here the word is meaningful but it still does not fit in the context with this meaning of 'doing'. We meet with a term similar in tone and context, with a slightly different spelling explained in detail in his work by HiuenTsiang.

**Krītya (Ki-li-to):** Hiuen Tsiang visited Kashmir in C.E. 631. His record describes three important interconnected topics on Kashmir: drying up of the land and emergence of Kashmir; origin of Buddhism in Kashmir and most important from our point of view, advent of the people named Krītya.

The Scholar-traveller writes: formerly the country was dragon lake. In old times the Lord Buddha was returning to the middle kingdom (India) after subduing a wicked spirit in Uddyana and when in mid air, just over this country, he addressed, Ananda thus: "After my Nirvana, the Arhat Madhyantika will found a kingdom in this land, preach to the people." In the fiftieth year after the Nirvana, the disciple of Ananda, Madhyantika, the Arhat, repaired to this country. He was sitting tranquilly in a wood on the top of a high mountain crag. The dragon beholding it was filled with a deep faith, and requested to know what he desired. The Arhat requested to give him a spot in the middle of the lake just big enough for his knees. On this the dragon withdrew the water so far, and gave him the spot. Then the Arhat founded 500 sanghararamas. He then set himself to procure by purchase from surrounding countries a number of poor people who might act as servitors to the priests.

"Madhyantika having died, these poor people constituted themselves rulers over the neighbouring countries. The people of surrounding countries despising these low born men, would not associate with them, and called them Krītyas, (Ki-li-to)," (Beal, 1884: Book-iii, 149-150).

Beal while translating the text explains the term krītyas in the note that the word in Chinese is given as Mai-te which is translated as 'bought people' and krītya is its equivalent term in Sanskrit, (Beal, 1884: Book-iv, 150, Note-94). Thus krītya is the right form of the term with its meaning 'bought' fitting in the context. Therefore the term in the work of Kalhan has to be read as krīta and the people designated by the term understood accordingly.

**The Krītya and the Kīra**: We now understand that the people referred in older times as Kṛtyas in the Rajatarangini are the same as

Krītya found in the descriptions of Hiuen Tsiang. Furthermore they are the same as those called Kīra in the Rajatarangini later and elsewhere. Cunningham affirms that the people named Krtya or Krītya are the same as Kīras. He writes, "Hwen Thsang states that the neighbouring kings held the base Kashmiris in such scorn that they refused all alliance with them, and gave them the name of Ki-li-to or Krityas, which would appear to be a term of contempt applied to evil minded and mischievous persons, as enemies, traitors, assassin, etc. The term which I have heard used is Kīr Mlechchhas, or the Barbarian Kīras", (Cunningham, 1924: 107). This explains the identification of the people known as Kīra and their nature. Here we observe that the ancient term Krītya in later times developed to Kīra and the two are the same people.

In a Sanskrit-Tibetan lexicon under the heading drag-po'i las-kyi bye-brag (= varieties of functions of the kind of people fierce) the Sanskrit term transcribed as *krītyā* is translated as gshed-byed i.e. executioner, giving it a new dimension, (rGya-mtsho, 1979: 24). It reveals its more archaic practical application.

Once Kashmir was known even by the name of Kīra. Gergan, writes that the Mons, a class of musicians, in Ladakh, know Kashmir by the name as 'Kyir,' (Gergan, 1976:631).

**Origin of Kīras in Kashmir:** As already stated above Madhyantika after founding the Doctrine procured by purchase from the surrounding countries a number of poor people to serve the priests. Other people called them as Krītya (Ki-li-to), a people bought. Thus the system was introduced into Kashmir by Madhyantika in the middle of third century B.C.E. This term and the system, however, existed already in the society in India. Madhyantika was a mere means of transfer.

Further developments in this respect are specific to Kashmir. Here in due course the literary term Krītya transformed to colloquial Kīra. We find earliest mention of the term in sixth century C.E. in the work of Varahmihira indicating to living in the same area. Further the aboriginal Krītya-Kīra people living in remote areas and of low social status ingenuously organised themselves into a strong group. They seized state powers and started ruling first over the small neighbouring countries and then they became kings of Kashmir. Their activities and name then expanded to other parts of the country. They were actively engaged in their traditional profession of combating even in twelfth century associating themselves with the kings of Kashmir, (VIII-2767). They made long leap in social development which is difficult to achieve even after great bloody coups.

Their expansion towards the north-east is available from the account of Francke. Francke states in his famous work Antiquities of Indian Tibet while giving the list of the rulers of Gilgit as "Kye-ris (Kiri)" and says that name is not available. Some travellers also mention similar name but no name is available. He also writes that "Kye-ris is claimed by the Gilgit Fards as one of their colonies."

## Krītyas in Ancient Indian Tradition

We find a similar word in the work of Monier-Williams as krītaka, also found used by others at some places, which is given as 'bought from his natural parents.' This leads to much older time in the origin of the system. Similarly a Hindi lexicon explains the term krīta as a people among the fifteen kinds of dasas, slaves, who have been made slave after purchasing.

Beal explains the term indicating to the existence of similar custom in the manner: the Krītyas or Krityas are defined to be 'demons who dig out corpses, or explained as serfs (persons bought, krita). They are said to be either Yakshakrityas or Manushakrityas, the former being shaped like Yakshas, the latter like human beings. The Manushakrityas were those domestic slaves whom Madhyantika introduced into Kasmir, (Beal, 1884: Book-iii, 156, note-119).

Regarding the origin of the system of slavery in India, Lakshman Sarup while translating the work Nighantu and Niruktawrites that, "The origin of slavery may be traced in the conquests of Aryans over the aborigines who represented a lower stage of organization, culture and refinement. They were easily subjected and being inferior in civilization to the Aryans naturally occupied the lowest place in the society. Thus all the ancient law-givers are unanimous in declaring that a sudra may be rightly reduced to slavery." In the classification he gives seven categories of slaves among which the fourth is 'he who is bought.' Thus the class of 'bought servants' existed in India much before its introduction into Kashmir.

**Kīras and Buddhism**: Kalhan shows Krityas as following Buddhism. From the descriptions of Hiuen Tsiang and as remarked by Cunningham the statement appears to be doubtful. As for the Krityas, as they had more than once been put down by the priests and their religion overturned, in lapse of time their enmity had increased so that they hated the law of Buddha, writes Hiuen Tsiang, (Beal, 1884: 157).

Cunningham remarks that, they (krityas) were extremely hostile to the Buddhists, who had frequently deprived them of power, and abolished their rights on which account, says the pilgrim, the king, who was then reigning, had but little faith in Buddha, (Cunningham, 1924: 106).

Hiuen Tsiang gives an instance that a king of Himatala punished the Kritya king of Kashmir by killing him for his having obtained the reign by overthrowing the king who followed the Buddha. Hiuen Tsiang writes, "After Kanishka's death the Kritya race again assumed the government, banished the priests, and overthrew religion." Evidently the Krityas or Kīras did not follow Buddhism.

### Kīras: The Kings of Kashmir

As regards the origin of the Krityas in Kashmir we observe that they were aboriginals, belonged to the remote areas of Kashmir and came from lowly social classes. In due course they organised themselves into a strong body and turned into a ruling class. They first ruled over the neighbouring areas of Kashmir. Thereafter as we learn from Hiuen Tsiang they became rulers over Kashmir itself. He gives an instance from the history of Kashmir relating that a king of Kritya ruled over Kashmir by overthrowing the king who followed Buddhism and then he was punished by the king of Himatala. He writes that, the king of Himatala (Tukhara) was by descent of the Sakya race. In the six hundredth year after the Nirvana of Buddha, he succeeded to the throne. He followed the Law of Buddha. Hearing that the Krityas had overthrown the law of Buddha, he assembled three thousand most warlike soldiers. Then under the pretence of being merchants laden with many articles of merchandise and with valuable goods, but having secretly concealed on their persons warlike instruments, they entered on this kingdom, and the king of the country received them as his guests with special honour. He then selected five hundred of these men of great courage and address, and armed them with swords and provided them with choice merchandise to offer to the king. Then the King of Himatala, flinging off his cap, proceeded towards the throne, the king of the Krityas, terrified, was at a loss what to do. Having cut off the king's head, the king of Himatala said to the officers standing below, I am the king of Himatala, belonging to Tukhara, I was grieved because this low caste ruler practise such outrages, therefore, I have today punished his crimes. Having banished the ministers in charge of the government to other states and pacified this country, he commanded the priests to return, and built a sangharama, and there settled them as in old time. Then he left the kingdom by the western pass. As for the Krityas after some years they came again into power, (Beal, 1884: Book-iii, 156-58). Here it is evident that the Krityas had begun ruling over the kingdom of Kashmir quite early and ruled for long time.

Beal quotes, "in the Visnu Purana it is said that, 'unregenerate tribes, barbarians and other Sudras will rule over the banks of the Indus and the regions of the Darvika, of the Chandrabhaga and of Kasmira."

## Kīras in Middle India

There are some inscriptional evidences containing the name Kīra available from Middle India. Scholars while translating the documents relate them to Kīragrāma. Kīras including those of Kīragrāma originally belonged to Kashmir.

These inscriptions also appear to indicate some linkage with Kashmir. One possible connection is through Lalitaditya Muktapida of Karakota dynasty who had conducted extensive campaigns in these regions expanding the Kashmir power. The inscriptions begin after about a century later than Lalitaditya's campaign and then extend to about three centuries thereafter. However, they belong to the same area where Lalitaditya had launched his campaigns. These evidences also cannot be related with any other power. This can be explained in the manner that the advent of the name Kīra in the region began with the campaign of Lalitaditya with whom the Kīras might have accompanied as combating forces. Then some groups may have stayed behind. They were joined by the others from the regions so that they became powerful and kept on organising campaigns. Such raids also might have been originating from Kashmir. There are some separate references to Kashmir also in the same documents.

Most of the texts in the documents show that the enemy Kīras, considered by all as powerful, have been defeated. The term has been used contemptuously. Whether it addresses a Kashmir power or any splinter Kīra group, we cannot judge. There are also references to the Rajas of Kīras.

The inscriptions belong to the period, as far as our knowledge goes, from ninth century to early twelfth century C.E. They do not mention any specific event or war won but give general information of victory of the writers over some states including the Kīras, which name always comes at the end of such lists.

For some reason the recurring references to Kīras in these documents appears to have prompted the scholars to assess them differently. Kielhorn remarks while translating some inscriptions that "in either case the writer probably thought more of his pun than of telling a real fact," (Kielhorn, 1896-97: Note: 246). The same view is repeated by Mirashi. The Kīras were ultimately defeated. Below we refer briefly some of the inscriptions.

**The Naga Karakota Dynasty:** The dynasty of 'Naga-Karakota' or 'Naga or Karakota' ruled over the kingdom of Kashmir for about two and half centuries, seventh through mid-ninth century C.E. The rule had been very strong. It launched imperialistic campaigns from Kashmir spreading to all the directions into most parts of India and outside India. Lalitaditya Muktapida was the star of the dynasty who devoted whole of his life leading conquests. This is the period when Kashmir expanded towards the Middle India.

The dynasty was founded by Durlabhavardhana who was son-in-law of his predecessor. Cunningham writes that he was of humble origin stated to have been the son of a Naga. A scholar writes that the Nagas were an aboriginal race of Turanian stock inhabiting the northern India. Naga is also a metaphoric reference to the dark-complexioned aboriginal tribes. The dynasty is also famous as Karakota. Sufi writes that Karakota occurs as the name of a presumably un-Aryan tribe. Thus we observe that the lineage originated from a socially weak class of aboriginal inhabitants. In the rise of the dynasty substantial contribution must have come from the Kīras who belonged to the same class of the society and they already had been ruling the kingdom. The belligerent Kīras may have constituted the fierce combating force of the regime. Naga, Karakota, Kīra and Sahi were rulers not much different from each other.

**Lalitaditya Muktapida and His Campaigns**: Lalitaditya Muktapida (695-732), son of Pratapaditya II, ruled more than 36 years. He passed his life chiefly on expeditions, wearing his own fame as head-dress.

Kalhan writes that the illustrious king Lalitaditya became the universal monarch of no bounds. This king who carried far his prowess abandoned his warlike fury only when the opposing kings discreetly folded their palms at his victorious onset. The king eager for conquests, passed chiefly on expeditions moving around the earth like the sun. The tribute from the eastern kings, the first great victory over Antarvedi, the land between Ganga and Yamuna, he took as his head-dress.

**Other victories recorded by Kalhan:** At Gadhipur in Kanyakubja he defeated the king Yasovarman and concluded a peace treaty which was broken and then the king was routed entirely. Then he moved towards the east. He subdued Kaling, Gaud, Karnata, Malaya mountain, Kaunkana, Dwarka and Vindhya. In the north-west, north and north-east outside India, he led conquests to Kamboja, Tukhara, over the Bhauttas, Darads, Town of Pragjyotish, Stri Rajya, and Uttarakuru. H.H. Wilson is appreciative of the accuracy in the geographical knowledge of Kalhan which is a confirmation of the authenticity of the author's descriptions in Rajatarangini.

Tripathi refers to a hoard of Lalitditya's coins discovered in district Banda, Uttra Pradesh and, refuting the proposition that the coins were issued from Kanauj, says that the hoard only may represent part of the treasure Lalitdaditya carried for the maintenance of his forces for his movement towards the east, (Tripathi, 1937: 203-4). In any way this is an authentication of the potential presence of the monarch in the region.

The famous Sun temple of Martand is attributed to Lalitaditya among the monumental works he executed in his kingdom. It is said that wine had been vice of Lalitaditya.

### Inscriptions from Middle India

i. **Khalimpur Plate of Dharmapaladeva:** The inscription was discovered in village Khalimpur, near Gaur, Maldah, West Bengal, and the date assigned is ninth century C.E.

   The inscription notes that, the king Dharmapala installed the illustrious king of Kanyakubja who really was accepted by the Bhoja, Matsya, Madra, Kuru, Yadu, Yavana, Avanti, Gandhara and Kira kings bowing down respectfully with their diadems trembling and for whom his own golden coronation jar was lifted up by the delighted elders of Panchala, (Kielhorn, 1896-97: 252). Here the inscription refers to a king of the Kiras.

   Majumdar, referring partially to Taranath, writes that the king of Kanyakubja referred to in the Khalimpur (West Bengal) copper-plate of Dharmapala c.770-810 A.D. is undoubtedly Chakrayudh. Taranath, Tibetan historian, writes about Dharmapala who built Vikramshila Vihara that, "He ruled for sixty-four years. He conquered also Kamarupa, Tirahuta, Gauda and other places. Thus his empire was very large and his command was extended in the east up to the sea, in the west up to De-li, [Delhi], in the north up to Jalandhara and in the south up to the heart of the Vindhyachala.... During the period of this king, western India was ruled by king Chakrayudha, which can be clearly seen in the brief inscription on the stone pillar of Jayasena. On a rough calculation, he [Dharmapala] was a contemporary of the Tibetan king Khri-srong-lde btsan," (= 755-797), (Chattopadhyaya, 1970: 274-276). The name Chakrayudha is retained by Taranath in Tibetan in original, untranslated.

ii. **Inscription from Khajuraho:** The stone inscription from Khajuraho of Yasovarman of the Vikrama year 1011 corresponding to C.E. 953-954 records erection of the temple of Vishnu, under the name of Vaikuntha, by the prince Yasovarman of the Chandela family.

According to the translator Yasovarman is represented in a general way as having carried on successful wars against the Gaudas, Khasas, Kosalas, Kashmiras, ...Yasovarman had received the image of Vaikuntha, which he put up in the temple founded by him from Devapala, the son of Herambpala. Herambapala in turn had obtained it from Sahi, the king of Kīra, who had received it from the Lord of Bhota, who again had got it from the Kailash. The inscription appears to have been set up after the death of Yasovarmana, writes Kielhorn, (Kielhorn, 1892a: 123-124). Here the king of the Kīras is named as Sahi, who received image of Vaikuntha from the Lord of Bhota.

iii. **Rewah Stone Inscription of the time of Kalachuri Karna, the (Chedi) year 800 equivalent to C.E. 1058-59:** Lakshmanaraja (945-970) (ancestor of Karna) is described as one who was clever in routing the king of ...... and whose foot-stool was honoured by the heroes of Kashmir, (Mirashi, 1937-38: 102).

Gangeyadeva (father of Karna) threw into the cage of a prison the king of Kīra who looked radiant with the mass of wealth of (the king of) Anga. Mirashi writes, "We do not of course know if Gangeyadeva succeeded in actually extending his dominions as far as the Kīra country which comprised the country round Baijnath in the east of Kangra District for victories over the king of Kīra country and even a pun on his name are found in other records which show that such descriptions more or less conventional," (Mirashi, 1937-38: 104-105).

The mention of the name Kīra here must be true. Baijnath colony of the community was small. They could provide assistance but the main force might have been from a different place.

iv. **Nagpur Stone Inscription of the Rulers of Malava, the (vikrama) year 1161, equivalent to C.E. 1104-1105:** Raja Lakshamavarmadeva of the Parmar rulers of Malva "being encamped on the banks of Vankshu, which were even softer than nature made them because the saffron-filaments on them were withering under the rolling of the teams of frisky horses, presented by the Turushka whom he had eradicated with ease, he taught the Kīra chief to utter most flattering speeches who on the account of the proximity of the Sarasvati was eloquent beyond measure, and whom was like a parrot shut up in the big cage", (Kielhorn, 1892c: 194). 'The Kīras are represented as having been held in check or defeated.' Here the poet metaphorically refers to Kashmir and then it alongwith Turushkas having been defeated.

v. **The Bhela-ghat Stone Inscription of Queen Alhanadevi, Dated (Chedi) 907, equivalent to C.E. 1155:** This inscription belongs to the time of Karna, son of Gangeyadeva. While this king (Karna) of unprecedented lustre, gave full play to his heroism, …the Vanga trembled with the Kalinga, the Kīra staid at home like a parrot in the cage, and the Huna left off being merry. 'Kīra were held in check,' (Kielhorn, 1892b: 15).

### Kīras in Modern Times

Kīras evolved their culture very early in Kashmir and stepped up to become a ruling class. They existed there in the third century B.C.E., sixth century C.E. in the time of Varahmihira, seventh in the time of HiuenTsiang and in the twelfth in the time of Kalhan. In Himachal they appeared earliest in c. C.E. 800.

In Madhya Pradesh (Central Province), it is stated that, "Kīra, a cultivation class, is found in Hoshangabad district. They numbered about 7000 persons in 1911. The Kirs claim to have come from the Jaipur State, and this is borne out by the fact that they retain a dialect of Marwar, though they have been living among the Hindi-speaking people of Hoshangabad for several generations. According to their traditions they immigrated into the Central Provinces when Raja Man was ruling at Jaipur. He was a contemporary of Akbar and died in A.D. 1615." They have 12 and half gotras. "Of the twelve names of gotras at least seven – Baman (Brahman), Bania, Mali, Mochi, Gadri (Gadria), Loharia and Jat – are derived from other castes, out of which seven are named occupational." This fact is sufficient to show that they are made up of recruits from different castes. "The caste worships especially Bhairon and Devi." "A peculiarity of the marriage ceremony is that the bridegroom is taken to the bride's house riding on buffalo. This custom is noteworthy since other Hindus will not usually ride on a buffalo, as being the animal on which Yama, the god of death, rides," (Russel, 1916: 481-483). Russel writes that the Kīras in Central Provinces are akin to Kirars and at the India Census of 1901 they were amalgamated with them.

There also existed a class of Kīra in Rajsthan: "A peculiar caste, Kir, very few in number, devotes its attention to the cultivation of melon," (Rajputana District Gazetteer, 1904:33). This may perhaps be a remnant group in its old social appearance having a different economic occupation in tradition now taking up a simple and innovative trade. We have no knowledge about the Kīras settled in Punjab and United Provinces (Uttar Pradesh). It is learnt from the people that there were large population of this class in Punjab and Haryana.

### Kīras in Himachal Pradesh in Modern Times

The term Kīra survives in Himachal Pradesh in memory as well as in practice but is little known. The tradition exists at two places in the two villages of Bharmaur in Chamba and Kummi in Mandi districts.

i. **Kīras in Bharmaur, Chamba:** Kīras had invaded Bharmaur and a number of their people might have got settled down there. The term survives in the village in memory and cultural inheritance. It is told that in the upper regions of the village there lived the people known as Kīra. It is told that they did not know farming. They had no knowledge of seasons. They settled where they would get good land. Evidently they were a migrating people. There is a saying about the Kīras which sums up their knowledge of agricultural practices. It says:

   *"kīrārī karṣāṇī, bāhaṇā peḍ ta hoṇā māṇī,"* (Ranpatiya, 2001: 22).

   It means that the farming of Kīras is such that they plant trees but in return get only the droppings of sheep and goat. This shows their ignorance and unfamiliarity with the kind of job done in the agricultural fields. These facts testify that the Kīras had lived in Bharmaur for quite sometime to have cultural interaction and leave its marks. There is a village named Kīrī in Mahla block in the district. A village with similar name is known to exist in district Shimla.

### ii. Kīras in Mandi

Kummi (Kummī) is a large village situated in tehsil Ballh, district Mandi, predominantly inhabited by a people called Kīra. It is situated about two kilometers away across Suketi Nala opposite to the town of Dadaur on the Mandi-Sundernagar part of the national highway and is well connected by metalled road. The residents divide the village into three parts: Uparla Kummi, Nichla Kummi and Bichla Kummi: the Upper i.e. eastern, the Lower i.e. western, and the Middle Kummi. The village lies, like those in the plains, on one edge of the large level plain called Ballh constituting fertile irrigated agricultural land. Therefore the view of its size and shape would not be available to a visitor.

Balh is a prosperous part of the valley of Suketi Khad, wholly plain, lying between the two towns of Mandi and Sundernagar, measuring about five kms. wide and fifteen kilometers long. Historically it lay between the old independent states of Mandi and Suket, now both being parts of district Mandi. Balh formerly formed part of Suket. It had been a bone of contention between the two neighbouring States and in their history many battles might have been fought on the issue as to who should own the golden bowl. It is the best part of the cultivated land of Mandi, its grain bowl. Suket lies at the south-west edge of the plain. Mandi town, the old capital of the state, lies some twenty kilometers away from the other edge of the plain. Kummi lies close on the border of the plain with Suket.

Ram Kishan (82, in 2020) retired as teacher and Tek Chand (72) retired from Police department belong to the village. Ram Kishan tells that their family belongs to Sisodiya clan. The residents of village Kummi are called Kīra. There are also people of their class settled in the nearby towns and villages viz. Dadaur, Seuri, Deura, etc. They have clans named: Belā, Kaṭāriyā, Gervī, Kogley, etc. Earlier they married only within the village. The other communities residing in the village are Julaha (weavers), Kumhar (potter), Koli, Saini, Brahmin, Thakur and Rajput.

They tell that they came from Punjab due to the breakout of plague there. People of their community are inhabited at Kurali, Ropar, Patiala, etc. in Punjab and Ambala in Haryana. They also tell that the Raja of Mandi made them to settle here and he also provided land to the settlers here. It is not known when they came from Punjab and who the Raja of Mandi was who gave land to them. But it appears wholly trustworthy that they were settled here by a Raja of Mandi.

There is no temple in the village or any kind of worship place. Their community goddess is Bālāsundrī who is enshrined in Kala Amb in district Sirmaur. They also revere Koyla Mata and Hatesvari Devi. They tell that they speak Mandiyali language. They have a different kind of language of their own which they are not able to tell. But they say that it resembles Rajsthani. They also tell that in the olden times they did the work of carrying salt from Mandi and they were called Lūngāra. Therefore they settled here. Kummi village lies in the Community Development Block of Balh. Below is given the outline statistics of the village according to the Census of 2011:

| | |
|---|---|
| Number of households: | 825 |
| Population : Persons: | 3938 |
| Male: | 1960 (50%) |
| Female: | 1978 (50%) |
| Scheduled Caste: Persons: | 3051(77%) |
| Male: | 1516 (50%) |
| Female: | 1535 (50%) |
| Litrerate: | 2802 (71%) |
| Male: | 1535 (55%) |
| Female: | 1267 (45%) |

The demographic statistics is ideal except that in respect of literacy they are somewhat lacking. According to local estimate by Tek Chand and Ram Kishan the number of households in the village are about 500 inhabited by about 3000 persons. 77% of the village population is scheduled caste. The official designation of the inhabitants is not known.

The pink-blackish rock salt of Mandi is of inferior quality. It is given that 25 to 38% of the material consists of sand. In Lahul and Kullu it was used only for use of cattle. White lake salt carried on the back of sheep and goats, which was used in kitchens, was brought by Lahulis from Jangthang down Rohtang pass and went further down. Salt also came from the Punjab.

The area of their settlement is prime land and is anybody's envy. They might have been given the area for their settlement by a Raja of Mandi, as they say themselves, to enable them to earn their regular livelihood. But Rajas would not gift grants for free. They might have been asked to win the land and then the grant was made for their fighting capability. They were then asked to live as a permanent force on guard of the state. Kummi is situated on the border with Suket.

**Summary**

The stone inscription from Khajuraho of Yasovarman of the year C.E. 953-954 records the name Sahi as the name of the king of Kīra. This indicates that the Sahis belonged to Kīra. Kīras thus established further kingdoms in the north-west India and were famed as Sahi. They ruled upto Afghanistan. They fought with Muhammad bin Kasim. They repelled the Arab invasions. Majumdar identifies them with the Sahi Rajas of Afghanistan stating that the Turkish Sahiya kings and Hindu Sahi kings are the same as Kīra-raja, (Majumdar, 1933: 11-17).

As the ancient system of independent small states started disappearing after the invasion of the forces from outside and they ruled under one umbrella their organisations got scattered. But as they were hereditary warriors they were welcome everywhere. They might have joined the Mughal forces and also joined the opposing forces of the Rajas. They are known to have fought under the Sikh Gurus. They might have fought like under Maharana Pratap.

Then they joined various classes of the society in various states. They adhered to different faiths and adopted varied professions: agriculture, trade, manufacturing, etc. Some of them appear not to have abandoned their ancestral professions. We cannot be sure, but we observe some families, among the roaming class, who might had been professional manufacturers of weapons of war, at many places still working on iron and their women, with good physique and looking strong, selling their home made articles like different kinds of axe, etc., on the road sides, although simple, but of common daily use of the rural people.

Some few others became serfs of liberty, in love of freedom. They, rather than changing themselves, live roaming, even though they had been mostly poor. They wander borderless in search of their homeland, lost long before. (Tobdan, 2022: 191-226).

# 8

# Hiuen Tsiang's *Mo-lo-so* and Other Countries Lying beyond Kuluta

Hiuen Tsiang, a great scholar and traveller came from China to India in search of Buddhist scriptures. In the Western Himalaya he reached in c. C.E. 645 the most interior point upto K'iu-lu-to, i.e. Ku-lu-ta of the ancient Sanskrit literature, and perhaps the present town and district of Kullu in the state of Himachal Pradesh.

## i. Lo-u-lo

From here, Kuluta, Hiuen Tsiang makes observation of the countries lying beyond in the northern direction and writes, "Going north from this, along a road thick with dangers and precipices, about 1800 or 1900 li, along mountains and valleys, we come to the country of Lo-u-lo (Lahul)," (Beal, 1884-Book-iv: 177). Beal in the text as well as in the note identifies Lo-u-lo with Lahul. Scholars identify this country with Lahul although there is some discrepancy observed in the distance which works out to c. 600 miles. However, Lo-u-lo is the exact transcription of the name Lahul which exists till the modern times.

Cunningham identifies Lo-u-lo with Lahul and states that, "To the north-east of Kulu, Hwen Thsang places the district of Lo-hu-lo which clearly is the Lho-yul of the Tibetans, and the Lahul of the people of Kulu and other neighbouring states," (Cunningham, 1924: 164). Cunningham treats the name Lo-u-lo as Lho-yul belonging to Tibetan language, meaning the southern district. Francke does not appear to agree with the suggestion fully. He writes that Lo-u-lo is meant for Lahul. But with respect to the Tibetan form of the name he writes that, "The Chinese name Lo-u-lo refers to Lahoul as the country is situated between Kulu and Ladakh. But

I cannot believe that Lahul is the Indian equivalent of a Tibetan word Lho-yul, 'south-land,' for I have never yet heard a Tibetan speaking of Lahul as Lho-yul. The name Lahul is used only by the people of Kulu," (Francke, 1908: 189). This term Lho-yul is not found in any other work or in use in any other manner. This name Lahul is used in colloquial, with changed pronunciations, in Kullu and Pangi, the neighbouring states of Lahul situated on its west and south.

This name Lahul is found inscribed in an inscription, obtained from Lahul, in Sharda script and Sanskrit language, (Tobdan, 2021: Plate 2). The inscription was read by Diwakar Nath Acharya who dates it to the period of ninth century C.E. The ancient form of the name Lahul is given as Lāhuṇa, (Courtesy Ane Nawang Jinba). We have no knowledge of its origin and the language to which it belongs. But the name Lahul is practically not used by the inhabitants of the area, in none of the four major linguistic-geographical cultures of Lahul. It is also not used by the inhabitants of the nebouring countries in the north and north-east.

It appears that this name was given at the time when rivers and other natural marks of Lahul were named by the missionaries of the emperor Asoka.

**ii. Mo-lo-so**

Hiuen Tsiang then goes on telling that, "North of this [Lo-u-lo] 2000 li or so, travelling by a road dangerous and precipitous where icy winds and flying snow (assault the traveller), we come to the country of Mo-lo-so (called also San-po-ho)."

Cunningham explains that, "Still further to the north he places the district of Mo-lo-so which from his position must certainly be Ladak. I would, therefore, alter the Chinese name to Mo-lo-po, which is an exact transcript of Mar-po, the actual name of the province of Ladak, as Mar-po-yul or the "Red district," in allusion to the general appearance of its soil and mountains," (Cunningham, 1924: 164). Beal in the note remarks that, "The suggestion of General Cunningham that Mo-lo-so should be read Mar-po (Mo-lo-po) is quite admissible." It is clear that Mo-lo-so as a country has been taken for Ladakh. We also agree with Cunningham that the term *Mo-lo-so* indicates 'Red district.'

Cunningham here takes the word Mo-lo-so equivalent to Mar-po or Mar-po-yul, 'Red district'. He says that this is the actual name of the district. He also gives the reason that Ladakh is known so "in allusion to the general appearance of its soil and mountains." This is a fact well known about Ladakh that it is also called red country. Cunningham has given reason for it. Thus comparing the word Mo-lo-so with Mar-po or Marpo-yul so far is agreeable. But here the exact transcription of the term *Mo-lo-so* is not available.

Tashi Rabgias, a historian from Ladakh, recounts the same fact and writes that,"Mar-yul is the ancient name of Ladakh, [by which he means red country]. This is so because the mountains of Ladakh are dmar-po, red. For this reason this country was named as "dMar-yul". The mountains are still red. During the time of Hiuen Tsiang also Ladakh was known as "dMar'yul." Mar-yul is the corrupt form of dMar-yul. Lotsaba Rinchhen Zangpo also constructed a Vihar at Nyar in Mar [Ladakh]," (Tashi Rabgias, 1984: 10-11). Thus Tashi Rabgias endorses that in the time of Hiuen Tsiang Ladakh was known as Mar-yul with the meaning as Red-country. We agree with Tashi Rabgias that Ladakh is designated as Mar-yul, red country.

Francke accepts Cunningham's proposition that the term Mo-lo-so stands for Ladakh. But he states that, "There is no necessity to write Mo-lo-po, instead of Mo-lo-so. The Chinese Mo-lo-so does not correspond to the Tibetan word mar-po, 'red' but to the Tibetan mar-sa, 'low land' (Mar occurs in the compound yar-mar, up and down)," (Francke, 1908: 188). Francke sticks to the original form of the word but he here gives different meaning to the word. It is different from that of Cunningham and Tashi Rabgias. Similarly Csoma in his dictionary translates Mar-yul as low land. This geographical feature of Ladakh has less relevance to the viewers of the land.

An old literary document preserves the name of Ladakh in its ancient form with proper spelling as dMar-yul, Red country. In one of the Namthars, biography, of Rinchhen Zangpo (958-1055), the Great Translator, it is given for Ladakh as dMar-yul i.e. Red Country. The text reads that, 'Then Vihars were constructed at Kha-chhar of Purang, Tho-ling of Guge and Nyar-ma of dMar-yul, [Ladakh], (Rinchhen Zangpo, 1977:90). Nyar-ma is located in Ladakh for which the term used is dMar-yul. The name appears in the work with this spelling at three places. This confirms that Ladakh is designated as red country. Although the sense as red country for Ladakh is known generally but the exact form of the name is not known. Francke, although differing in meaning, gives the original form of the word in sound.

Thus gathering from the explanations given by the different scholars as above we conclude that the former part *Mo-lo* of the term Mo-lo-so stands definitely for dMar, red. The second part *so* stands for '*s*' meaning 'land, place.' Thus the full term Mo-lo-so is equivalent to dMar-sa [d in dMar remains always silent] which means Red-land. This name in Bhoti is derived from one of the principal geographical feature of Ladakh as given above by the various authors. Hiuen Tsiang's Mo-lo-so is exact rendering of dMar-sa, Red-land, the earliest name known of Ladakh. It appears that the ancient and original form of the name got lost before the time of Rinchhen Zangpo. It is also possible that taking the name dMar-sa as folk form, it was changed to literary form, maintaining its original sense, as dMar-yul. Practically the people then took for use the literary form of the name. Literary form in Bhoti also might have started coming from the time thereabout.

Petech states that geographically Mo-lo-so stands for Ladakh, but he finds 'serious philological difficulties in transcribing the names.' He further writes that, "In my opinion Tibetan Mar-sa is quite impossible. First of all such a name would imply that the language spoken in Ladakh in the early 7th century was Tibetan which is in a high degree unlikely, not to say impossible," (Petech, 1977: 7). Petech has also another reason for rejection of the proposed reading and suggests a different reading. The simple answer to the objection is that it is right that the reading dMar-sa, meaning Red Land, is undoubtedly Tibetan, however, it may be presumed that it is a name given for Ladakh by the people living outside Ladakh. Thus it would not be necessary to know about the language spoken in Ladakh at the time.

### iii. San-po-ho

Hiuen Tsiang, as seen above, gives the term for Ladakh fully as "Mo-lo-so (called also San-po-ho)." Thus it explains that Mo-lo-so is also known by another name as San-po-ho. The translators explain that in a note to the original text it is remarked that the country is also known as San-po-ho. Beal gives a note to the main text as, "The country is also called San-po-ho." Petech also notes, "An original note to the text remarks, (Mo-lo-so) is also called San-po-ho," (Petech, 1977:7). Thomas Watters, another translator, also gives the same statement. These narrations indicate that the two names are connected but loosely. Thus scholars take San-po-ho as synonym for Mo-lo-so.

Alexander Cunningham explains that the other name San-pho-ho is a literal transcription of Tsang-po, or the river, 'which is a common designation for Indus in Ladak, and in fact for any great river in the Tibetan language; San-pho-ho is, therefore, the country on the Tsang-po, or Indus," (Cunningham, 1854: 4). Francke is agreeable with the suggestion. But we generally find that when a river is sometimes found named after the name of the country, it is found generally named so for the portion through which it flows, or sometimes for whole of its length. River takes the name of the town or the country. Petech leaves the issue undecided.

Hiuen Tsiang then refers to the same name San-po-ho again. This time the name is stated alone. He appears to have gained the information that the country San-po-ho instead of being synonym of Mo-lo-so, is a separate country. Thus he tells its location from a different position, from the side of Guge. He writes that, "This country [Brahmapura] is bounded on the north by the great Snowy Mountains, in the midst of which is the country called Su-fa-la-na-kiu-ta-lo (Suvrnagotra). From this country comes a superior sort of gold and hence the name. ..... On the west side this country is bordered by San-po-ho (Sampaha or Malasa (?))," (Beal, 1884-Book-iv: 198-199). This country of Suvrnagotra, as known at the time of Asoka, is identified with the present country of Guge, (Tobdan, 2021: 44ff.). Hiuen Tsiang gives the name San-po-ho here alone and tells that it is bordered with Guge. This indicates that the country is different from Ladakh and is independent although it lies along Ladakh as he has mentioned Mo-lo-so and San-po-ho together earlier. According to the Traveller this country lies west of Guge but along Ladakh. Hiuen Tsiang is so particular that he has taken Zanskar as a separate country.

Zanskar lies exactly at such a position. Zanskar is situated between Lahul and Ladakh. The ancient description of Hiuen Tsiang applies to Zanskar fully. Cunningham describing its geography writes that: "Zanskar lies in the general direction of south-east to north-west along the Zanskar river. On its north lies Ladak and on the south lies Lahul," (Cunningham, 1924:21). Zanskar lies slightly to the west and the land between Lahul and Ladakh, having three snowy high passes and route with a distance of seven days journey on foot, is uninhabited. On the east of this lies Rubsho and Jangthang, parts of Ladakh and it borders with Guge. Rubsho is very thinly populated area and Jangthang is mainly pasture land. Thus San-po-ho agrees both in the form of the word and geographically with Zanskar. In Bhoti, it is written as Zangs-mkhar or bZangs-dkar.

Zanskar culturally is an advanced country and is known since ancient times. In the time of the Great Translator Rinchhen Zangpo there were Translators from Zanskar who worked in translating works from Sanskrit, with the Indian Panditas, into Tibetan. One of them was renowned as Zankhar Lotsaba, Translator from Zankar, (Tobdan: 1987: 81-85).

There were famed Lama writers from the area. In the family of Nawang Tshering, there appeared lama-writers in two or three successive generations from one family. Csoma de Koros, the renowned earliest European scholar of Tibetan stayed in Zanskar studying Tibetan and Buddhism.

# 9

# Tibetan Pilgrims Going to Jalandhara and Uddiyana: Their Route in Himachal Pradesh

Jalandhara, modern Kangra, and Uddiyana or Urgyan were the famous pilgrimage places of Indian Buddhism in India for the Tibetan pilgrims. The practice of Tibetan pilgrimage kept the history of the places live for longer period in the medieval times in the north and north-west India after the disappearance of the Faith from the areas. Uddiyana, after long debate, is finally identified with Swat Valley now in Pakistan. North West India, which includes Urgyan, had been famous in Indian history since ancient times for many reasons. Panini, the great Sanskrit grammarian, belonged to the region. It was famous in the tradition of early Indian Buddhism surviving in the Gandhara Art. Arya Asang and Vasubandhu, the two brothers, belonging to Purushapura, Peshawar, were great scholars of Mahayana Yogacharya. Yogacharya and Tantrik Buddhism spread from here. In Tibetan tradition Urgyan is known as the birthplace of Guru Padmasambhava, the Vajrayan Acharya.

There were also born some famous siddhas. Those among the famous 84 siddhas are: La-va-pa, i.e. Kambalipada, Indrabhuti, his sister Lakshminkara and Jalandharipada - the king of Jalandhara. The region was famous for the production of wool since ancient times. Agrawala tells that Panini makes mention of kambala-karakas, blanket-makers, who produced several kinds of woollen blankets. Kambalipada, one wearing blanket, a great siddha, belonging to the same area but to much later period, must have acquired the epithet for the same reason. This indicates that the activity of production of wool and manufacture of the woollen articles in the area was still live.

Padmasambhava, the native of Urgyan, who also has relationship with Zahor i.e. Riwalsar, Mandi, Himachal Pradesh, carried the practice of Vajrayana to Tibet and became famous there. Tibet has great regard for the Teacher and the place of his birth. The place, therefore, has been regarded as a great pilgrimage place.

D.C. Sircar writes that mention of Uddiyana is found made in the Hevajratantra during the time of Gopala, of Bengal, in the middle of the eighth century C.E, recording an earlier tradition, as a pitha, holy place, among the four viz.: 1. Jalandhara, 2. Oddiyana or Uddiyana, 3. Puranagiri and 4. Kamarupa. This list has now got expanded and the number of holy places or pithas number twenty-four and they have been placed according to the parts of Vajrabody, Vajrakaya. Urgyan also is included in this list. sTag-tshang Raspa writes it also as the place of the dakinis. Uddiyana had great attraction for the siddhas from Tibet for pilgrimage as one of the most sacred places equivalent to or next to Bodhgaya.

## Pilgrims' Route

The pilgrims coming from Tibet first reached Guge. From there they entered India at the head of Kinnaur through Shipki La. Further they followed the same route which was commonly used by the local commuters constituting the traders, pilgrims and the common people. From there they came to Spiti and then to Lahul. They spent some time on the way at some places, more in Lahul. From Lahul along Chandrabhaga they went to Pangi. From there across Sach Pass they entered Chamba and then they reached at Jalandhara. This is the route followed by almost all the pilgrims going to Jalandhara. Those going further to Uddiyana went either from Jalandhara or straight from Chamba and Nurpur to further.

The inhabitants of Kinnaur, Spiti and Lahul were well acquainted with Guge and its products of merchandise. The traders from these areas went carrying goods like grains, cotton cloths, sugar, etc. every year to Guge and in exchange they brought wool, salt, pashmina, borax, etc. This enterprise was carried on at a large scale and regularly on annual basis since long past. The pilgrims followed the same well known and safe route.

While coming from Spiti one has to cross Kunzom pass, lying between Spiti and Lahul. Presently, after crossing the pass, as one reaches the bank of the river Chandra, his path leads him along the river as it flows and reaches at Khoksar in Lahul. The traditional route was different. After crossing the pass the traveller, instead of going down, went up along the river, passing through close by the Chandratal, crossed Baralacha pass and entered Lahul. In Lahul one travelled along the Bhaga and then Chandrabhaga and entered into Pangi. It was the requirement of the pilgrims that, as far as possible, they should travel in cool climate and favourable cultural geography. This route was suitable for them till the end, Jalandhara.

On the way they found Lahul as the most suitable place where they liked to stay for much longer time. The leading three pilgrims each stayed in Lahul for more than a year. In Lahul they found some rich monuments and sacred places. They visited and stayed in the important sacred places of Gandhala, Kuluta-Gushal, Rebag-Avalokitesvara and Maru-Margul.

In Pangi above the line of the original settlements along the right bank of the river, along the whole valley there are the settlements of the later immigrants who are called Bhot locally and their settlements as Bhotaur. The large and well known Bhotaurs are, starting from nearest to Miyar Nala in Lahul: Chasak, Hilutuwan, Kumar, Parmar, Hundan and Sural. These are names of the villages of the original settlers and the immigrant settlements lying above them are named as such with the addition of the term Bhotaur. Thus Chasak Bhotaur, etc. There are also five monasteries there. The pilgrims might have had advantageous interaction with them.

Going from Pangi, immediately after crossing Sach pass and on entering Chamba there is a village named Bhanodi situated at a distance of about 12 kms. from the top of the pass, on the west, on the right side of the traveller. About three kilometers above the village, at a lonely place, there is a monastery affiliated to Tibetan Buddhism. The establishment is new but it stands at a place where there existed a bubbling institution in the former times. The old structure was deserted and it has now been founded again. This must have been founded by the pilgrims for taking rest after the long and tiresome journey and gain energy for further journey. Thereafter they went crossing the valley of Churah to Chamba town and then they moved on to Jalandhara or Nurpur, then to Uddiyana.

### The Pilgrims

Two siddhas, Urgyanpa (1230-1309) and sTag-tshang Ras-pa (1574-1651), successfully completed their pilgrimage to Urgyan. The two, for this reason, are famous as Urgyanpa. There are a few more names associated with the pilgrimage. They accomplished the journey partially i.e. upto Jalandhara. Gozangpa (1189-1258) was the teacher of Urgyanpa. He came upto Jalandhara and spent about four years in completing the jounrey.

Indeed he was the pathbreaker and he inspired the would be Urgyanpas and others. The path became clearly known upto Jalandhara. Rang-rig Ras-chhen (1595-1683) of Spiti and Nawang Tshering (1657-1730) of Zanskar are other two renowned siddhas who also visited Jalandhara.

### 1. Gozangpa (1189-1258)

Gozangpa (rGyal-ba rGod-tshang-pa), thinking of going to Jalandhara (Dsva-lan-dha-ra) came from Zhang-zhung etc., to Spiti, (pi-ti bi-lchog). In the north of Spiti he met a great siddha named Kha-rag-pa who had not risen from the position of meditation for thirty years. He met some more sturdy siddhas. Gozangpa asked from the one, "I wish to go to Jalandhara. Is there any obstacle?"

Then he came to Lahul (Gar-sha). There is the mountain named Gan-dha-la. There is a flat land equal to one dpag (= 24,000 feet app.). On the peak of that mountain he saw a self-born chaitya named dharma-murti (dharma-mutri), image of the Doctrine. There are the real products of water and wood. This is the holy place blessed by the Virs, Heroes, of the Doctrine, and the Dakinis. There reside many male and female saints for accomplishing their siddhi, meditation.

'Specially there is a place of pilgrimage dedicated to Avalokitesvara ('Phags-pa) [Triloknath]. I wished to stay there [at Gandhala] during the winter. Due to heavy snow there was no cave. There were caves for meditators in the winter but these were occupied by the great meditators and there was none vacant. There was a household like a monastery but I did not wish to stay there.' I came to 'Gar Lotsha-ba and told him about going to Jalandhara.'

The Teacher told, 'You cannot go. There is scarcity of provisions. You don't know the language. There are many robbers on the way who can kill you. Even if you reach in India, 'I have heard' there are non-human spirits at the cemeteries there who create obstructions.'

'The gold I had was consumed at Kailash (Tise). So I said, 'I don't have.' There he gave provisions for the way. He also provided an interpreter.' A Minister of the king of Chamba named Su-tu accompanied with the two Siddhas.

'Then after three days going from Lahul reached a high snowy pass [Sach ?]. In appearance it was like a glass touching the sky. Thinking how to go there, there were many Monpa [Mon, the local people] carrying loads.' Then after eleven days they reached the Mon-Yul, country of the Mons. The mountains and valleys were narrow and the path lay through jungle. The Mons were wearing only animal skins. Then in twelve days they reached the capital of Chamba. There all the mountains of Monyul come to an end. There starts the plains of India which is level like the plain of palm.

'We told the king that we are going to Jalandhara for meditation.' He met king Bi-tse-kra-ma having seven thousand ministers. From Chamba to Jalandhara it took him to travel three days. Jalandhara is one of the twenty four sacred places. The land is plain like the palm, pleasant and prosperous.

There flow two rivers and at the junction there is the rock which is like an elephant sleeping. There is the settlement named Nā -ga ko-ṭa (Na-ga ko-tre) having large number of inhabitants. On the nose of the mountain there is the Vihar of Jawalamukhi (dsva-la mu-gi). I visited the place. I also visited Bha-ga-su.

"Nā-ga ko-ṭe in Tibetan means castle of serpents. There I stayed for about five months. Then I went to Tibet, by a short route," (Gozangpa: 80-96).

The Teacher states that he met the king of Chamba named Bi-tse-kra-ma. This king may be identified with Vijay Varman who sat on throne in C.E. 1175 but his later date is not known. Gozangpa was in Chamba in around 1215. There appears some possibility of meeting of the two.

Gozangpa spent four years in completing the journey to Jalandhar, from the age of 26 to 29, from C.E. 1214 to 1217. He stayed more than a year in Lahul. There is a cave named Gozang Phug above Silla gonpa which falls in Tinan valley. There is a village named Gozang, across Kyelang. These all must be related to the Great Teacher.

### 2. Urgyanpa (1230-1309)

Urgyanpa (Urgyan Seng-ge dPal) took his journey to Urgyan in the early second half of the thirteenth century. He came to Ruthog in the winter and stayed there. Then the three brothers of Jo-bo, the Chief, of village gLang-'Khor paid visit to him. They asked for prophecy for their lost turquoise.

In Ruthog he came to be known as the reverened Lama of the Jo-bo of the village gLang-'Khor. Then walking the distance of seven day's walk of an ordinary person in one day he came to the pilgrimage places of Ku-lu-ta [Gushal, in Lahul] and Ma-ru [Margul] i.e. Lahul. Kuluta and Maru are among the 24 great pilgrimage places, equivalent to the knee and thumbs of feet of Vajrabody.

'I had no tiring and fatigue in the body and mind. The Guardian Lady of the Land, the great pilgrimage place, there flowed red fluid of pus and blood from her nose. She said, 'You don't stay with the Teacher. You do not stay in the company of the friends. You don't go anywhere and stay here. I will provide you the articles of necessity. But in the mind I had the thought of going to Urgyan. I did not go to Urgyan that year.

'At Gandhala (Ghan-dha-la) I sat in meditation. I washed away all the dirt of evil thoughts. With the clean and empty mind I consumed all the elixirs of the Doctrine.

'In the summer I stayed there at mount Gandhala. There grow many excellent medicinal plants. There are five springs of water where there flow the water of accomplishment. At the holy place there is a good follower who meditates on the Teacher rGya-ras-pa. He is named as rGya-rgod.' Urgyanpa also delivered many sermons in Lahul relating to the different thoughts. of the Doctrine.

'At Gandhala there is the Guardian of the Land named Na-ga-de-ba having a turquoise in her neck with great bright shining. She is the Dakini of knowledge. At mount Gandhala there grow in the soil medicinal plants of three hundred and sixty varieties. There is the thick jungle of growth of the essential plant of ru-rta, costus. I did not take even single piece of ru-tha. This is the chief of the collections of the men alienated from the worldly affairs.'

Then he went to Jalandhara where he got prophecy from a siddha in the Nagarjuna cave, (rTa-mgrin, 1997: 54-63).

The journal indicates that Urgyanpa from Ruthog came straight to Lahul. This we learn from the statement that, 'walking the distance of seven day's walk of an ordinary person in one day' he came to Ku-lu-ta and Ma-ru.' He knew the route well from Gozangpa, his teacher. He does not name Kinnaur and Spiti but he came past these two regions. Urgyanpa also stayed in Lahul for more than a year.

In the monastery of Chhukutsi, sTod, Lahul, there is a very simple, small image of Urgyanpa, with typical round cap, which is the symbol of Urgyan, (Tobdan, 2021: 299, Plate - 17). This is the only image of the Teacher known to us in the region.

### 3. sTag-tshang Raspa (1574-1651)

sTag-tshang Raspa (Ngag-dbang rGya-mtsho) came to be called as the Second Urgyanpa. He visited Uddiyana under the most difficult conditions, nearly impossible. But his determination was unshakable. He went twice in 1613 halfway upto Balakot and 1615.

The travelogue of sTag-tshang Raspa is in detail and is much informative. The Teacher also appears to be much adventurous. For the first time when he came from Tibet, after crossing the Shipki La, instead of adopting the usual traditional route as described above, he chose the shorter and much difficult route, from the angle of climate, and went down through the Satluj valley. After crossing Kinnaur and Rampur he went crossing the river Satluj to Suket, probably through Karsog, then to Jawalamukhi and further. The pilgrim also appears to have been a bit in hurry, may be due to the shortage of time, as the hot summer season was fast approaching. He went but had to come back from Balanath Tila, due to the lack of physical endurance of his companions.

He writes the title of his Travelogue to Uddiyana as, "A-o-rgyan mKha'-'gro'-i' gLing-gi Lam-yig." It may be translated as 'The Travelogue to Aorgyan – the Land of Padmasambhava - inhabited by the Dakinis.' It gives significance to the land on two counts, as the birthplace of Padmasambhava and as the land where there reside the Dakinis. He gives the account of his journey in his Namthar, Biography, and Lamyig, Travelogue. We give description from Namthar and Lamyig separately. We give the account of his journey to Uddiyana covering the part falling in Himachal Pradesh. The two documents although narrate the same subjects but they differ somewhat in detail. So they are complementary.

sTag-tshang Ras-pa was mostly alone in Urgyan. He was constantly under threat of life and remained always in stress. At the moment he meditated on his teacher and lightened his burden of mental stress. During this period he had to mostly converse in Hindi. He has recorded some dialogues in Hindi. spoken by the others to him and his answers. These have been edited and translated, (Tobdan, 2021a:160-169).

#### a. Namthar

In 1613, sTag-tshang Ras-pa [Tiger-den Mendicant] took circumambulation of the lake Mansarovar and the snowy mount Tise, Kailash. Passing through the middle of Guge, crossed Ship-ki pass (?) (Sha-ram La), He visited Pu-li-ra-ma-la (?), a holy place among the 24 countries. From the village of Shyaso (Sha), in the country of Kinnaur (Khu-nu) came to the pilgrimage place of Jalandhara. At Kangra (Nā-ga-ko-ṭa) he stayed for about half a month. At the junction of the two rivers he clearly viewed the image of the Jogini. At Jalandhara there were many Tibetan pilgrims. They returned fearing the heat saying that by the first month [Tibetan Calender, i.e. Feb.-March] saffron starts flowering and then the hot summer also begins. So saying the other Tibetans returned. This Lord stayed on. He was alone. The three companions did not agree. He requested them to stay together. Then the four companions going quickly in ten days reached Balanath (Ba-la-na) Ti-la. They visited Autre and Rameshvara. The three companions insisted to visit the places of Khri-brtan and Pushpa-hari [two places mentioned in the Namthar of Rinchhen Zangpo] in Kashmir. The friends became sick and told to return to Tibet. The Lord himself came through the way on snow travelling for fifteen days and then reached in Zanskar.

There was the Mahasiddha bDe-ba rGya-mtsho. Then he stayed at Zongkhul, in the cave of meditation of Naropa. Then there reached also the friends who had come from Naga-kota. There came an invitation from 'Jam-dbyangs rNam-rgyal, the King of Ladakh, Mang-yul. He sent reply, "I am a pauper roaming distant lands. I salute none other than the Three Precious Ones." At 'Bar-gdan Mahasiddha bDe-ba rGya-mtsho arranged teachings to the followers.

Then he came to Lahul (Garzha), the Land of Dakinis. The kings Tshering and dPal-sde, etc., gave services. He gave teachings [at Khangsar] to Sonam, the younger sister [reference by the speaker] [wife] of the Chief and the disciples. "In Lahul I stayed for one year."

He started his [2nd] journey to Uddiyana in the first half of the eighth month of Tibetan Calendar, nearly October of 1615.

He was ready to go alone. Zhi-ba rNam-rgyal, a disciple of the Teacher said himself to come as attendant. "We made an agreement of no responsibility and no help." From Darcha (Dar-rtse) they came to Khangsar, Kyelang (sKye-nang), Ku-lu-ta in Gus Mandala [Gushal], Maru [Margul], Ka-ma-ru [Rebag, Triloknath, where there is the image of Avalokitesvara of rdo-ka-ma-ru, marble], Chamba city and Hindustan, Nu-ru-phu, Shri-na-ga-ra, etc., (sTag-tshang Raspa-i, 23b-25b).

**b. Lamyig**

Firstly the Teacher describes geographical location of the holy place and then the significance of the sacred place of Urgyan.

Uddiyana is the holy place where the excellent great siddhas receive siddhi, accomplishment. It is situated approximately 2,273 miles (500 dPag-tshad) away from Vajrasana, Bodhgaya, in Magadha. There the king Indrabhuti became disciple of the Buddha alongwith his family members. creating the practice of the Maha Guhya. Leaving the mortal body he attained the body of the Rainbow.

'Gro-ba Drang-srong 'Bugs-'byin [Jagata Munī Āśvāsa (yati) (?)], incarnation of Vajradhara, and La-va-pa [Kambalīpād], etc. many Mahasiddhas and noble men were born here. It is on the way to Ka-ma-la Pir as it is called in vernacular by the Indians.

From the Snowy Tise, Kailash, the place from where the four rivers of Jambudvipa originate, he came to the village of Khyung-lung, iṇ Guge, in the country of Zhang-zhung. Coming from Guge, in five days reached Shipki pass (Sha-ram La). On crossing the Pass he reached at the head of the valley of Kinnaur, Khunu. From there he came to Namgya (rNam-rgyal), Pu and Shyaso (Sha). From there in two days reached Sarahan (So-ra-ra) and Khyagsu (?). From there in five days reached at Suket (Suge-thang), [Karsog?]. From there in three days reached Jawalamukhi. There fire burns on stone and water. Nagarjuna offered fire sacrifice for both these sites. It is told that nearby there is a rock, like the shape of belley, the meditation cave of Nagarjuna, which could not be found.

Then came to Kang-kra ko-ṭ [Kangra-kot], a very pleasant place. Although the King of the place is Buddhist, there reside followers of both faiths of Sanyasi and Jogi. From Kang-kra-koṭ, he went towards the west for a day. Then came to Nu-ru-phu [Nurpur], Shrinagara, Pathanan, No-sa-ra, Ka-thu-hara, Ba-ru-rd, Pa-tha-na Mu-sur, Sa-ki-ri, Sa-lo, Ghe-tshar, Bhur, Sa-la-kothu and So-ta Ko-ta. From Gho-tsa-raka, in two days reached Ba-la-na-ga-ra Tila. There live the class of the Jogis.

Then they came to Kashmir (Kha-chhe). There were three companions. They were worried of the heat. They told to help them to go back to Tibet. Therefore they came to Kashmir. This is the country where Naropa was born. This is like the finger, among the 24 countries and still held by the Buddhists. Then he reached Waran [= Maru Wardwan?].

Then walking for fifteen days [from Kishtwar] on snow and crossing a snowy pass reached Zanskar. He stayed in a monastery where there lived Siddha bDe-ba rGya-mtsho. He stayed for two months at Zongkhul in the cave of Naropa. The companions coming from Nagarkot reached there. There was invitation to come to Lahul. Then went to 'Bar-gdan. Sermons were given to Siddha bDe-bar Gya-mtsho.

Then in sTod, Lahul, the king Tshe-ring dPal-lde served for about three months. Then at Khangsar younger sister [reference] bSod-nams, mother and son [mother of, the ruling chief], did serve well. He gave explanations on history, Mani ka-bum [a book], etc. Sister bSod-nams did herself much religious studies. He went on pilgrimage to mount Gandhala, Gus Mandala, Re-phag, Margul, etc, and visited many holy places in the mountains. In the winter stayed at the monastery of gYur-rdsong [Beeling] in meditation for six months. In the Spring gave explanations on Khrid at bKra-shis Shug-lung [Shashur gonpa, Kyelang]. Then the king Tshering dPal-lde invited him to Rang-yo. He stayed at Dar-rtse for about two months. In all it had been one year in Lahul. He left the other companions there. The Teacher had a disciple who insisted to accompany him. "We two made an agreement. [Based on the experience he had previously with the three companions.] It is better if we two make an agreement. If you become sick, I will go breaking the rules of the lama leaving you. You will be left wherever you are. I will go wherever I reach. If I am not able to go further you can go leaving me there." From Dartse they reached at Khangsar and Kyelang. At Gus Mandala there is the knee Kuluta. From there in two days reached Rephag, Triloknath. There is Avalokitesvara, the liberator of the six kinds of beings, symbol of Knowledge. Actually there is a stone image of Marble. Then in one day reached mThe-bong Ma-ru, Margul, the thumb. Then in one day reached Pa-ta-na, i.e. Pa-ta-nam, Miyar Nala. Then they reached the top of the Ko-ta-la [Ko-ta = Ghordhar; la = pass] pass. Crossing that great snowy pass, reached Pangi. Then reached at Sural (Su-ra). Then in two days reached Na-ran (?). It is known as the country of armpit among the twenty four countries. Then crossed a great pass [Sach]. In two days held the head of the valley of Chamba. Then in seven days crossing that valley reached the plains of Hindustan. Then went to Nu-ru-phu, Shri-na-ga-ra, Pa-tha-nhnha, No-sa-ra, Kathu-ha-ra, Ba-tu-ra.

**Note:** When sTag-tshang Raspa came back from Balanath Tila on his first visit he came to Kishtwar in Kashmir. He walked on snow for fifteen days and passed either the Phoat La or Umasi La and reached Bardan gonpa in Zanskar where there was residing siddha bDe-ba rGya-mtsho who later on patronized the Shashur Gonpa near Kyelang. (sTag-tshang Raspa -i, Namthar: 1a-6a).

**Kangra:** Gozangpa gives the earliest form of the name of the modern Kangra which in one form was famous as Jalandhara. The Teacher calls it at one place as Nāg-ko-ṭre and at another as Nāg-ko-ṭ. Both forms are transcriptions of Nāgakoṭar in Sanskrit. The Teacher translates the name as klu-mkhar, castle of serpents, which is an exact translation of the Sanskrit Nāgakoṭar, hollows of serpents. It means that it is the place of habitation of serpents. The great rock face standing at the junction of the two rivers– Banganga and Majhi - rises straight up on the face of which there might be numerous hollows inhabited by innumerable snakes which caused the place to be named as such. At the top of the rock is situated the renowned ancient fort of Kangra. Urgyanpa writes the name in slightly different form as Na-k-r-kro-tre i.e. Nāgarkoṭar, but it records the original form of the name.

sTagtshang Raspa names the place as Nāg-ko-ṭ [Fort of Serpents] and Kang-kra-ko-ṭ. The original name Nāga-koṭara of the time of Gozangpa has now got changed. sTag-tshang Ras-pa rather records the mid development of the name as Nāga-ko-ṭa and the forerunner of the existing name as Kāng-grā-ko-ṭa. Thus by this time the new form of the name, which is in use presently, had originated.

Thus the name Kangra can be put from its origin to the present form as: Nāga-koṭara ~ Nāga-ko-ṭa ~ Kāṅ-gaḷā-ko-ṭa ~ Kāṅgḷā ~ Kangra.

### 4. Nawang Tshering (1657-1730)

Nawang Tshering (Ngag-dbangTshe-ring) came from Padar to Pang-ge, as he writes for Pangi, in c. 1684-85. In Pangi he reached at Ghan-dhar(?). Then he was at Sural. Here, at the place of Phag-mo Gru-pa (1110-1170) he met Mahasidh Kur-kur. Nawang Tshering was asked to stay there. But he told that he was on pilgrimage. From here he went to Jalandhara, but he did not go through Sach pass.

### The Route of the Pilgrims through Lahul and Pangi

sTag-tshang Ras-pa, in the second time went through Lahul and Pangi. He instead of going along the valley, went from Udaipur up along Miyar Nala, about four miles, turned towards Pangi and crossed the Ghordhar pass, and then he shows himself in Sural, at the top end of Pangi valley, above Kilar. Immediately after crossing the Ghordhar pass in the midway there is the Chask Bhotaur.

**Ghordhar Pass:** Pangi was geographically a naturally protected land. Communication within Pangi itself and with the outside territories was extremely difficult. Here mules were not used in the past. Pangi could be approached from three sides. Firstly it could be reached from the two ends of the valley of Chandrabhaga, i.e. from Lahul in the north-east and Padar in Kishtwar in the south-west. The easiest route was across Sach pass from Chamba, which was difficult but was not as dangerous.

About the road linking Lahul with Pangi, Cleghorn writes, "The only communication in Pangi are narrow rugged tracks, running along either bank according to the mountain slope is favourable. Many parts overhanging the rivers are almost impassable for a laden man and between Salgrain and Madgrain, especially the difficulties are such that even dogs and unladen sheep must be carried," (Cleghorn, 1864: 146).

Vogel writes about the pass, "An ancient route connecting Pangi and Lahul leads up the Saichu Nala to the Chandrabhaga valley which it rejoins at Markula or Udaipur. Starting from Sach the stages are Saichu (8,412'), Baraut (11,638'), Singhmarh (13,000'), Miyar (10,215') and Chimra[t]. This road notwithstanding the pass is said to be shorter and easier than that which follows the Chandrabhaga. It is practicable for hill ponies which circumstance accounts for the name of the pass," (Vogel, 1911: 216).

This pass is formed over a spur emanating from the Zanskar range, the northern barrier of Pangi valley, and ends at the right bank of Chandrabhaga. It lies between Miyar Nala in Lahul and Saichu Nala in the middle of Pangi. Its height is 16,300 feet. It generally remained covered with snow.

## Tibetan Pilgrims and the Monasteries in Chamba dedicated to Tibetan Buddhism

There are two monasteries in district Chamba dedicated to Tibetan Buddhism located on the other side of the Pangi Range towards the Chamba town. These are Jasoorgarh and Bhanodi located in the villages of the same name, both in Churah valley.

### i. Jasoorgarh Gonpa

The village Jasoorgarh is situated at about three hours' journey by bus from Chamba town. The monastery is situated at a distance from the village approachable on foot diagonally downwards for more than half an hour. The whole area is slopy but there are fields and houses. The monastery is known after the name of the village as 'Jasoorgarh Gonpa,' but its literary name is bSam-gtan Chhos-gLing. This monastery is supported by the residents of the village. They are immigrants from Kinnaur who might have come in around C.E. 1850 in connection with, as is said, once the famous sapphire business. The occupation erupted in Kishtwar in J & K and had attracted people from distant lands like Ladakh, Lahul, Kinnaur, etc. They founded the monastery.

The building of the monastery is a one room, single storey, longitudinal, of about 20x10 feet dimension. There is a verandah all along the front wall of about six feet wide running along the whole length of 20 feet. The building is covered with slanting roof of thin local stone slate. There is a large lawn before the building. There is no insignia of monastery outside like dar-chhen (long flag staff), chhorten or inscribed manye stones.

The entrance to the hall is at the right end. As one enters the hall one can see that along the back wall there is a cement slab laid all along about two feet wide at the height of two feet from the ground. The images are placed on it in single row. It appears that the building was originally built with some other purpose later on it was converted to gonpa.

The central figure is of Avalokitesvara in standing posture, about four feet in height, of six arms, the two in namaskar attitude. On the left is the image of Amitabh and further left is of the Buddha. On the right side is that of Padmasambhava. All the three are in sitting posture. The monastery belongs as such to Nyingma – Dukpa-Kargyud tradition. The images were constructed by a Kinnauri artist. The gonpa can be estimated to have been founded in around C.E. 1900. The principal image matches with that at Bhanodi and are contemporaneous having been built by the same Kinnauri artist in c. middle of the twentieth century.

The monastery celebrates the Tshechu festival, the birthday of Guru Padmasambhava, every year on the tenth of the first month of the Tibetan Calender. It is celebrated on the lawn in front of the monastery. Men and women sing and dance in a circle holding hand with hand, maintaining the Kinnauri tradition. Jasoorgarh is off the main route and is not connected with the Chamba-Pangi highway. The place has no relationship with the pilgrims going to Jalandhara or Urgyan.

### ii. Bhanodi Gonpa

While coming from the side of Pangi, soon after crossing the Sach pass there comes after some distance a village named Bhanodi where there is also a gonpa nearby the village. On the side of Chamba, between Chamba and Sach pass, Bhanodi, in the Churah valley, is the last village from the side of Chamba and the first from Sach pass, situated on the ancient highway linking the two places, which was covered on foot.

The building of the gonpa is of two storeys high of one room at each level, with a verandah in the front and is covered with slanting slate roof. It looks like a local residential house. Presently it is run by the Khampa residents who have some uncultivated land here. They are not agriculturists. They are settled in Chamba town where they earn their livelihood by doing business. In 2016 there was an old Khampa Lama named Sonam Gyatsho, of about 70 years, incharge of the monastery. Around the monastery there is no other residential house, and none between the monastery and the village. The monastery was reestablished recently. Before this there might been some ruins of an old building. No particular name is known of it.

### mChhod-khang: The Worship Room

The principal statue in the monastery is of Guru Padmasambhava. The attitude of the image presented here is unconventional. It is placed on a high raised altar about four feet high and the large image, of human size, is in sitting posture with the large right leg stretching forth. The first look a viewer gets is of the sole of the shoe of the image and the face of the image is at a distance in the back. Left hand holds a large bowl and the right hand resting on the knee is in teaching attitude. On its (viewer) right side is an image in standing posture, coloured wholly red, crowned with a row of skulls, appears to be a guardian deity in wrathful attitude. On the extreme right is Avalokitesvara, about four feet high, in standing attitude, in the form of thousand arms. Six arms are apparent, of which the two foremost are in Namaskar attitude. The image in all aspects is similar to that at Jasoorgarh.

Yeshe Dorje tells that these images were constructed by an artist from Kinnaur about a hundred years before which may be placed at c. C.E. 1900. The artist has clearly left some impressions of his native land on his creations.

Inside the monastery there is nothing to indicate its antiquity. But there is one unrelated small image. On the left of the Guru, beside the right foot, there is a small naked female image. Its head is empty having a thin layer of cropped curly hair. Head is slightly bent towards its left and is looking down. The ornamented ears are large. Left hand is raised in front of the chest, holding something. Around the palm a necklace is seen. A large necklace passing over the right shoulder goes towards the back under the left arm above the waist. There is a strip of waistband. The rear part of the arms near the joint wear large round plain and thick four or five rings. Below the waist the image is hidden behind an object. This may be an old Indian sample. The image has no relationship with the group and has no relevance here. It does not belong to the class of the deities placed on the altar.

Outside the monastery, at a distance of about 10-15 feet, there is constructed a small structure on which are placed some old manye stones, round and about half a dozen slabs, collected and placed over it. The writings on the slabs are inscribed very beautifully. They are all religious. They reveal their antiquity. These old engravings indicate the presence of a religious establishment formerly here. We don't find the name of the place referred in the Namthars of the travelling lamas. The two leading persons connected with the monastery are Swarandeepak Raina and Yeshe Dorje.

**Tibetan Inscriptions from Bharmaur**

Vogel records a Tibetan inscription which he found on the bank of Brahmi river about two kilometers from Bharmaur towards Chamba which reads as, 'khyung-po jo-nu 'phags-pas' which is translated by A.H. Francke as 'the august younger prince of the Garud Lords,' (Vogel, 1911: 252-3). Here in the inscription if we read it as it is, it can be translated as 'by Arya Garuda Thakur.' In this manner from the word jo-nu' we have used the former part jo (=Thakur) but then the other part is left as redundant. Therefore it should be read as gzhon-nu (=Kumar, prince). Thus the changed lettering of the inscription would have been: "khyung-po gzhon-nu 'phagas-pas." Thus it can be translated as 'This inscription was written "by Arya Kumar Garuda' or 'by Arya Kumar Khyungpo".

Two inscriptions in Tibetan are reported to have been found in Bharmaur. One of them was found in village Goshen, on a rock below the village. There are five sentences in it and all are very common sacred formulas. The lines look still fresh and clearly legible although it appears to be considerably old. As we read from the photograph published by K.P. Sharma (2001, plate No. 17), the five sentences are: (i) aum maṇipadme hum. (ii) aum vajrasattva hum, (written thrice). (iii) aum ā hum. The letter 'A', the first letter of the first word in all the five sentences is subjoined uniformly below it by the small 'a'. There are two stone inscriptions in Bhoti placed in the Bhuri Singh Museum at Chamba. All these indicate to the activities of the pilgrims.

**Bhanodi: The Halting Station**

The village of Bhanodi lies on the ancient route linking Chamba, the capital of Chamba State, and Kilar, the headquarters of Pangi Wazarat. The pilgrims coming from Sach pass could reach here in half a day. The monastery might have been built at this unfamiliar place by the pilgrims with the view of benefit for the pilgrims. Later on some of them perhaps got permanently settled here in the village.

The route passing through this village was short but difficult. It was the route of the accustomed and habitual travellers. Therefore it was difficult and at places also risky for the travellers unaccustomed to walk on such high hilly routes. An ordinary Pangwal could cover the full journey from Chamba to Kilar just in two days for which the others needed three or four days.

Pal Singh, 1961, describing the stages of the route from Chamba to Kilar writes that, "Starting from Tarella the first halting station is Bhanodi at a distance of 6 miles. It is situated at a height of 8,550 feet. Besides a few houses of local inhabitants this place is mostly inhabited by the Bhotes. A small tea-cum-snacks stall caters to the needs of the travellers," (Pal Singh, 1961: 2). During this period the last bus terminus from Chamba was Tissa. From there onwards the journey to Kilar had to be undertaken on foot.

The Gazetteer of district Chamba, 1963, notes that the distance between Chamba and Kilar by the old road is 68 miles (109 kms.) and by the new vehicular road existing between Chamba and Tisa, it is 103 miles (165 kms.).

Prabhat Sharma travelled in 1986 and mentions the stations on the route as: Alwas, Bhanodi, Mukhaha-pharh Nala, and Satrundi, the base camp for Sach pass, (Prabhat Sharma : 2016: 162-163).

Minakshi Chaudhry, 1998, writes that, after Tarella the first halting station is Bhanodi located at about 10 kms. This place is inhabited by Bhots. There are a couple of seasonal hotels and tea stalls at Bhanodi.

Travellers halt for night at Bhanodi also. Normally people prefer reaching Satrundi on the same day after starting from Tarella. After Bhanodi the path goes through thick forest of oak and pine. It meets with the motorable route at Satrundi, (Minakshi Chaudhry, 1998: 137-145).

Thus Bhanodi was a halting station for the commuters between Chamba and Killar till around 1990. Thereafter as the bus route was constructed the village fell off the route.

The ancient route and the modern bus route bifurcate at Tarela and meet at Satrundi. Minakshi Chaudhry gives the distance from Tarela to Satrundi through Bhanodi as 17 kms. and the distance by the bus route today between the two stations is 30 kms. This route thus reduced the distance by more than ten kilometers between these two stations.

The pilgrims used the place most probably for more than simple halting. They took rest for a few days in order to regain the lost energy and gather for the further journey. For return journey they perhaps adopted some different routes in order to visit new places. By this time they had also become somewhat acclimatised.

**Rinchen Zangpo: The Pathfinder**

Before the start of the continuum of pilgrimage of the Tibetan devotees of Buddhism to north and north-western India the route was set out by the Great Translator Rinchen Zangpo (Rin-chhenb Zang-po, 958-1055). He, a native of Guge, adjacent to Kinnaur and Spiti, went to Kashmir in C.E. 975 to study Sanskrit and Buddhism through Kinnaur (Khunu) and Lahul (Gar-zha), as is stated in his Namthar, and certainly through Pangi and Kishtwar.

The Namthar of the Translator reads an incident that, 'When he was in the seventeenth year of his age, a pandita came from Urgyan to his house. His mother offered him a rug to sit and then served him meal. When the guest had left and the mother removed the rug, she found a beautiful book left out under it. Rinchhen Zangpo looked at it and said that he could not read the Indian script but he thought it must contain some good instructions. In the sleep he had a dream in which a dakini made revelation to him about Kashmir.'

Rinchen Zangpo decided, "I will go to Kashmir. This time I will not go to eastern India. Then he requested Tashi Tsemo (bKra-shis Tse-mo), his elder brother, to be his companion and guide."

'In the eighteenth year of his age [in C.E. 975] he started his journey from his native land. He took with him about 600 cowrie shells, articles of necessity, delicious food - preparations of his mother - ration and some tattered clothes. He had with him as a companion his elder brother Tashi Tsemo and a guide, a Mon from Nyungti [a native of Kullu].

"We went begging alms from Khunu to Garzha. Then in a month and three days reached in a village named Ka-ri-ka. There the Nyungtipa, the companion from Kullu, worried of walking did not wish to come. Then we two, the Lord and myself, went on. Walking for three days we reached at a place where there was the Mahansangala [maha-sanga], so named a big bridge. We gave fifty cowries and spent one night with worry,' (Rinchhen Zangpo, 1977:68).

Although here we may identify Ka-ri-ka with Kilar in Pangi, because it appears to be natural, but at that time Kilar was not yet a settled place. But there is no doubt that the Great Translator went from Lahul to Pangi and through Pangi passed towards Kishtwar. The route was natural and suitable. The term Mon, means in Tibetan an inhabitant of the Himalaya, the regions lying between Tibet and the Indian plains. Here it means a resident of Kullu, Nyungti.

The travellers crossed a bridge and there they paid some fees. Here it is necessary to note the kind of currency used and acceptable in all the nations the travellers traversed. In Kishtwar valley, which lay on their route, there existed such a point till the nineteenth-twentieth century.

There over the bridge for crossing the river Chandrabhaga or Chenab there were posted regularly some workers for the maintenance and safe conduct of the passengers and their baggages for which a small amount of fees was levied. We are not aware of such an example elsewhere in the whole region of western Himalaya. The Gazetteer of Kashmir and Ladak, 1890, and the other old Gazetteers of Kashmir, describe about Doda in Kishtwar as such a place. This may be identified with the place as mentioned by our travellers. It gives as follows:

"Doda: Lat. 33° 9'. Long. 75°36'. A town in the province of Kishtwar situated on a small plain above the right bank of the Chandra Bhaga river, it lies at the foot, and partly on the slopes of a grass-covered hill, bare of trees.

'The town itself is surrounded by trees, a few willows and poplars mingled among hundreds of fruit trees give it shade and beauty. About half a mile below the south end of the town, the Chenab roars in a swollen and turbulent flood. The sides of the river are very rocky, and for some feet perpendicular, that on the right bank is the most precipitous, for there being only room for a hut and two stunted trees, on the bare ledge of rock above the bridge, on the left bank the ground shelves, and there are a few huts, and a baoli [pool] shaded by trees.'The suspension bridge which is of the chika description swings at a high elevation above the torrent, here above 50 yards wide; the transit of passengers and luggage is a tedious, though not really a dangerous operation.

'There a regular establishment is maintained to work the bridge and a small amount is levied on each passenger and passage passed across.

'During the months of June, July and August, consequent on the melting of the snows, the river rises considerably, the bridge has then to be moved to a higher position," (Gazetteer of Kashmir and Ladak, 1890: 294).

Chika here may be explained as the kind of traditional bridge of thick woven twig rope. In village Tinno, sTod, Lahul, such a bridge of birch twigs, over river Bhaga, which was repaired every year, was known as 'Shika zampa – Shika bridge.'

Thus Rinchhen Zangpo had already travelled through the greater part of the route of the later pilgrims and had shown the way to them.

# 10

# Approaches to Pangi: A Historical Review

Pangi is a sub-division of district Chamba. It lies in the valley of river Chandrabhaga. In the same valley on its south-west lies the region of Kishtwar in Jammu and Kashmir and on the other end of Pangi, in the north-east, lies Lahul. Pangi is connected with Chamba town through Sach pass across the Pangi Range which lies between Chamba and Pangi. Between Pangi and Chamba there are also a few other passes through which people cross often. The geographical features of the three divisions within the valley of Chandrabhaga differed very much from each other. Within Pangi the communication was difficult due to tough topography. The narrow valley is filled with precipitous rocks and thick jungles. Kishtwar is relatively wide and the valley is slightly open and there is less obstruction of jungles. Lahul is slightly wider, rocks are not so obstructive and there are very less jungles. The communication with Pangi from both sides was extremely difficult in the ancient times.

Pangi traditionally was approached from three directions: Kishtwar, Lahul and Chamba across the Sach pass. Communication with Chamba was essential because Pangi was part of Chamba State. This route although quite long but was easiest among all the three. Communication with the other two regions was natural and of necessity.

### i. Kishtwar

About the route between Kilar, the headquarters of Pangi, and Kishtwar, the Chamba State Gazetteer 1904 reports that there is a Jhula over the Ganaur/Sansari Nala which forms border between Pangi and Padar. As such ponies and laden sheep could not pass through the route. Yet there was cultural relations and regular intercourse between the inhabitants of Pangi and Padar of all kinds but only to a limited extent.

Hutchison (1923) gives detailed description of the route from Kilar to Kishtwar (Kashtwar) as follows. From Kilar the road runs down the right bank of the Chandra Bhaga at a high level. Near Darwas (7 miles) there is a steep descent to cross the Sural Nala and then a more gradual one to the jhula over the Sansari Nala, which is the Chamba boundary. Rising steeply the road runs on to Ashdhri (12 miles), and then again descends to cross the Angai Nala and further on the Kaban Nala at Sol (12 miles). This stage is rough. From Sol to Gulabgarh or Atholi (8 miles) the road is fairly good. From Gulabgarh a branch ascends the Bhutna Nala and crosses the Umasi Pass (17,400 feet) to Padam in Zanskar. The main road to Kishtwar crosses to the left bank of the Chandra Bhaga at Padar, (Hutchison 1923: 33-34).

This road in 1923 was quite difficult. Over the Sansari Nala there was a bridge which is called Jhula, a traditional suspension bridge made of twisted twig ropes. It was not worth for the passage of laden sheep and ponies.

Prabhat Sharma (1986) relates the stages existing on the present motorable road from Pathankot to Kilar as:- Pathankot, Jammu, Patnitop, Batot, Doda, Thathri, Kishtwar, Atholi, Gulabgarh, Sohal, Tayaari, Sansari Nala, Dharwas and Kilar. The distance from Kishtwar to Kilar is 120 kms.

Presently Kilar is linked with Jammu by a motorable road. This road was linked sometime around 2005. Thereafter this route was used for about four-five or more years by the travellers from Lahul for going to Kullu via Jammu and Pathankot due to early snowfall on Rohtang pass and its early closure. Deepak, a taxi owner, carried the passengers between Kullu and Lahul via this route for three years from 2009 to 2011. He tells that the road was then kutcha and the condition was such that if the Tata-Sumo vehicle had luggage on its roof even slightly higher, then it would touch the roof of the rock on the way.

**ii. Pangi and Lahul:** The road linking Pangi and Lahul ran through the main valley of Pangi. The Gazeteer of 1904 writes that, 'The main road in Pangi is a continuation of that from Kashtwar and Padar and enters Pangi at the Jhula over the Sansari Nala. Rising to Darwas it crosses the Sural Nala and runs up in Pangi. the right bank of the Chandrabhaga, at a high level, to Kilar.'

Cleghorn, the earliest to write on the subject, reports about the condition of the road which linked Lahul with Pangi that, "The only communication in Pangi are narrow rugged tracks, running along either bank according as the mountain slope is favourable. Many parts overhanging the river are almost impassable for a laden man and between Salgrain and Madgrain, especially the difficulties are such that even dogs and unladen sheep must be carried," (Cleghorn, 1864: 146). Very limited amount of goods could pass through the route.

Smith still three decades thereafter writes that, "There is one main route in Pangi which follows the course of the river and connects the valley with British Lahoul on one side and Padar on the other. In places it is a mere track running along either bank as the slope happens to be favourable and is so bad in parts that without seeing, it is not even easy to conceive of a thoroughfare so difficult and dangerous. The worst part is between Salgraon and Madgraona," (Smith, 1891: 75).

Cleghorn mentions the stages of journey between Triloknath in Lahul and Darwas in Pangi as follows:

| Name of the Stages | Dist. Miles | Remarks |
|---|---|---|
| Triloknath | – | – |
| Madgrain | 9 | Cross Bendee and Chandrabhaga by wooden bridge. |
| Salgrain | 12 | Path very dangerous, impracticable for ponies, and sheep, laden coolies must proceed with care. |
| Tindi | 10 | The Drati pass leads to Tindi. |
| Rowlee | 9 | – |
| Tathialla | 8 | – |
| Shor | 6 | A frail twig bridge. |
| Parti | 6 | – |
| Raee | 6 | – |
| Sauch | 9 | Path very bad. Opposite Cheni pass. |
| Sidh | 9 | – |
| Kilar | 6 | Headquarters of forest officer, opposite Sach pass. |
| Darwas | 12 | A large village near the frontier of Raja of Chamba. Path tolerable. |

(Cleghorn, 1864: 152).

It gives a distance of 102 miles from Triloknath to Darwas covered in 12 stages. Only men with load on the back could pass through the path but he too had to be very careful. Cleghorn uses a word 'Bendee' at the first entry at Madgraon. 'Bendee' in Pattani language means river. We can take it here also for bridge. Cleghorn gives the road running from both the banks of the river. We can broadly put here that from Madgraon to Rauli the road ran on the right side of the river. Then it crossed to left and again at Shaur crossed to right and then it continued on the same side upto the border with Paddar.

Hutchison (1923) gives the details of the path as follows: "After leaving Kilar the road crosses the Hunan stream and gradually drops to the bank of the main river at Siddh-ka-dera. It then enters a narrow chasm where the planks, forming the roadway, are supported on iron bars fixed in the cliff. The Parmaur and Saichu Nalas are crossed near Cheri, the next stage, on the river bank below Sach (8 miles). At Mindhal bridge the road crosses to the left bank and runs almost level to Purthi (10 miles). The Cheni and Shilal streams are bridged by trangaris and on a rock near the latter stream are the glacial markings. At Purthi the road crosses the river by a jhula to reach the forest rest-house; the main road running on past Ajog to the jhula at Shor (4 miles).

'From Shor to Tindi is two marches and no change at Rauli. The road which is difficult in places follows the left bank at a high level to Tothal, a small flat opposite the Karun Nala. Beyond Tothal it runs along the face of a precipice over-hanging the Chandra Bhaga to Rauli (9 miles) and most of the way is narrow and dangerous; but between Rauli and Tindi (7 miles), it is fairly good. From Tindi to the Harser Nala is an open flat, but the rest of the way to Silgraon (8 miles) is along the face of the cliff and somewhat difficult. At Silgraon the road crosses to the right bank, and except at the Kurcher Na1a, and one other spot, is narrow and dangerous all the way to the Darer Nala near Margraon. At Margraon (12 miles) the Urgad Nala is crossed, and from this point the valley is open and the road good. At Udaipur the Miyar Nala is crossed by a wooden bridge, and Triloknath (6 miles) on the left bank, is reached by a bridge over the main river. Another bridge above Triloknath carries the road back to the right bank, along which it runs to the Chamba border at Tirot and then to Jarma (14 miles) in British Lahul. The Tirot Nala is crossed by a wooden bridge. Road good all the way from Margraon, and fit for ponies," (Hutchison: 1923: 34-36).

This route was extremely difficult and also dangerous. From the description of Hutchison as above, we learn that the road coming from

Kilar crossed to the left bank of the river at Mindhal bridge. Then it crossed back to the right bank at Salgraon. Then it continued further on the same side.

The distances shown by Cleghorn between the two stations are longer for all the stages from those of Hutchison from which it appears that earlier the paths were more circuitous and later on some improvements were affected and the paths then became shorter.

The Gazetteer of 1904 writes that, Ponies and laden animals come down the main valley as far as Madgraon; below this point the roads are passable only for sheep, which are utilized to carry grain, salt, etc., to and from different places in the valley and over the passes in the Pangi Range to Chamba. The road might have been improved sometime before this as at the time of Cleghorn laden sheep could not pass through this route.

**Ghurdhar Pass:** Between Miyar Nala in Lahul and Saichu Nala in Pangi there is a pass (16,300') over the spur which originates from the Zanskar range and ends at the right bank of Chandrabhaga. A path led across this pass through which loaded ponies were brought from Lahul to Pangi. For the same reason, perhaps writes Vogel, the pass was named as Ghordhar[Horse Range]. The pass had to be used in the olden times because laden animals could not go through the main path along the river.

### III. Chamba to Kilar

The Pangi Village Survey Report 1961 writes that among the three routes the most commonly used route was that from Chamba which remained open during the summer months from June onwards. The route was quite long but not difficult as much as the other two. From the descriptions of the different writers belonging to different periods we learn that the passage and length of the route kept on changing. This might have been caused by the improvements done from time to time on the route and occasional change in the alignment of the road.

i. Gazetteer of 1904 provides that the Pangi road on leaving Chamba descends to the Sal Nala which it crosses to reach the right bank of the Ravi. At Kiyani it leaves the river and ascends a ravine to Pukhri, on the watershed between the Ravi and the Siul. Continuing to rise to Masrund it drops by a steep descent to cross the Karair Nala, and again rising winds along the slopes overhanging the Siul to the rest-house at Kalhel. Here it descends to cross the Kalhel stream, and regaining its former elevation runs on the level till it drops again to the Nakror bridge where it crosses the Chanju Nala. It then winds along the slopes for some distance and crossing the Tisa Nala ascends to Tisa. From the top of the ridge above Tisa the road, gradually descends to the Baira Nala which it crosses at Guari. It then runs up the Alwas Nala to Tharela, and a few miles on reaches Alwas. Here coolies are engaged for the Sach Pass, which is crossed in three marches to Kilar in Pangi. The intermediate stages are Sitrundi and Donei or Bindraban. Near Dhid the road enters the main Pangi Valley, and crossing the Chandrabbaga by a wooden bridge ascends to Kilar.

The Pangi road is good all the way, except for the toilsome ascents and descents at the different tributaries of the Siul. Ponies can go as far as Alwas and may cross the pass in July, and later, but are of little use in Pangi. Laden animals can go as far as Tisa; but are not usually taken beyond Masrund, (Gazetteer, 1904: 249).

ii. The team of the Census of India, for the Village Survey in Pangi, in 1961, journeyed from Chamba to Kilar and they have left recorded their experience. Starting from Chamba the bus dropped the team at its last station at Tissa, the headquarters of Chaurah Tehsil, at a distance of 43 miles from Chamba.

The next station Tarela is situated at a distance of 12 miles where one has to travel on foot and the goods are carried on mules. It is the base business centre for supply of commodities to Pangi. Here there are five shops dealing in grocery and general merchandise. There is no Rest House here. The shopkeepers arrange for the night stay of the travellers. The mule track ends here and further journey has to be undertaken on foot. Though Kilar is only 33 miles the journey is most tiring and at places dangerous.

From Tarela the next halting station is Bhanodi situated at a height of 8,550 feet at a distance of 6 miles. A small tea-cum-snack stall caters to the needs of the travellers. After Bhanodi the next halt is at Satrundi at the height of 11,000 feet. It is also the base camp for the Sach pass ascent. We started in the early morning for the ascent to Sach Pass, 3 miles, above from Satrundi. But the onward journey upto Dunai is too tiring. One has to walk on glaciers and rocks. After crossing the Sach Pass the downward journey is mostly in steep descents and sometimes in slight ascents continues.

An image of goddess Bhagwati has been erected at the gulley on the pass by the local people. After half a mile below the Pass there is an open space of nearly 15,000 feet in area. A heavy rock lying on one side of the ground is said to represent a Rakshas, demon. Dunai is the next halting station, being 12 miles away from Satrundi. It is situated at a height of 10,100 feet. There is a small building of two rooms under the charge of the dak-runner [one who carried postal bags from one post to another]. While going to Chamba it serves as a base camp for Sach pass. Chandrabhaga is crossed by a shaky and dilapidated suspension bridge which is so rickety that it starts swinging and swaying. To reach Kilar, on the way a number of small bridges known as trangaris have to he crossed.

The total distance is 88 miles (Chamba-Tissa - 43; Trela - 12; Kilar-33), 141kms. Their halts were at Tarela, Bhanodi, Satrundi and Dunai and then reached Kilar. They covered the journey in five days, (Pal Singh, 1961: 2-4).

iii. Prabhat Sharma (1986) covered the journey from Chamba to Kilar in two days, partly in vehicle. 'We started journey from Chamba in the early morning by an official vehicle on July 21, 1986 and reached Tarela. From there the team started journey on foot and crossed Alwas, Bhanodi, Muhjahapharh Nala and lastly reached Satrundi. This is the base camp for ascent to Sach pass. There is a hut built under a big boulder which was termed as rest-house by the people staying there. There were mats filled with cotton placed over dry twigs with leaves which kept on pricking the whole night. The cotton in the mat had rolled to balls. Over it was placed a coloured bed sheet. There was a blanket and a quilt filled with cotton which similarly had turned to balls. There was a tea vender, a Sherpa youngman, nearby, who also served meal.

'Next day, we covered the ascent of five kilometers in three hours and reached Sach Pass where there was a Gorkha youngman who had a tea shop. Then we reached Bagoto. There is a tent of the Gorkha tea vender. There was a shed raised under a boulder. After taking tea we reached Dunai. There is a rest house like that at Satrundi. Then we reached Bindrabani. There is a rest house, different from the previous two, and also office of a junior engineer. It had a building and it was roofed with wooden planks rather than tin. We moved to

Kilar. On the Chandrabhaga there was a Jhula drawn on a wire and pulled by another person on the other side. We reached Kilar in two days with only one halt on the way.' The normal period of journey is four days and the halts are at Tarela, Satrundi, Bindrabani and then reaches Kilar, (Prabhat Sharma, 2016: 162-168).

iv. Minakshi Chaudhry (1998) gives some more information. She writes that a Pangwal would cover the distance between Chamba and Kilar in two days. The road was then motorable upto Bairagarh. There was jeepable road upto Satrundi but at the time it could go only upto Kalaban. There was a bridge over Chandrabhaga river, (Minakshi Chaudhry 1998: 137-145).

In 2023 Pangi is well connected by motorable road from all the three directions. The road from the side of Lahul was the first to be opened in 1996. The work on the road the side of Udaipur had started in 1990. The road from the side of Kishtwar was opened a few years thereafter, c. 2005. The road between Chamba and Kilar was the last to open in the year 2008.

After the opening of the Rohtang Atal Tunnel in 2019, the obstruction of the Rohtang pass has been reduced very much. The tunnel has rather become an object of great attraction for the commuters and the tourists. The road connecting Kilar with Kullu through Lahul has become much convenient. It has greatly affected the utility and importance of the Chamba-Kilar road. It has made the transport of goods between Kullu and Pangi faster and cheaper. It has also made the Manali to Jammu route through Lahul and Pangi more functional and beneficial. The road remains open during the winter also with occasional closures for short periods owing to snowfall.

From the descriptions as given by various authors belonging to different periods we have come across four kinds of bridges. In 1904 there was a wooden bridge over the Chandrabhaga river. In 1961 there was a rickety swinging bridge. It was perhaps wooden bridge hanging over steel wire ropes. In 1986 there was a box suspending from a wire rope with wheels and drawn by another persons sitting across. These days it is known as Jhula. The Village Survey Report 1961 mentions *Trangris* found between Chandrabhaga and Kilar. These are local bridges laid over small nallahas.Two or more tree trunks are laid across the nallah. Over it are placed wooden planks or stone slabs.

# 11

## **Lahul:** Its Different Names

The sub-division of Lahul, district Lahul-Spiti, is situated at the head of river Chandrabhaga. It constitutes three valleys of Chandra, locally known as Tinan; Bhaga, the upper part known as sTod and the lower part as Gahar or Punan; and the combined valley of Chandrabhaga called Manchhad, Melogs or Pattan. The sub-division is known by three different names as Lahul, Gar-zha and Songla (Songlā). Origin and literal meaning is known about none of them. Of the three names the first, the name Lahul, is not used by any of the linguistic-geographical society of Lahul.

I. **Songla:** Songla, signifying the whole Lahul, is a name used by the people of Pattan or those who use Pattani language. A section of the society who know themselves as brahmins are also called Songla.

II. **Garzha:** The inhabitants of the Upper Part of Lahul, i.e. the valleys of Chandra and Bhaga, know Lahul as Garzha. Outside Lahul the regions lying on the northern side like Zanskar, Ladakh, Rubsho and Spiti know it as Garzha. In Tibetan the same term is used but with some variation both in literature and verbally.

Some scholars, presuming it as originating from Tibetan language, have attempted to explain it. Francke suggests that Garzha is made up of two original names: a'-zha, signifying an ancient tribe, and dkar-zhva, meaning 'white cap', (Francke, 1926: 279). Gergan suggests that it is the corrupt form of dkar-zhva, (Gergan, 1976: 330). As far as the first part of the name i.e. a'-zha, signifying a tribe inhabiting the Chinese Turkistan in Central Asia, is concerned, Lahulis do not appear to have any relationship with them except that there is some nearness in the forms of their names.

As regards the second part of the name dkar-zhva, the assumption of the two scholars is apparently based on the analogy of Tibetan names for

India and China as rGya-dkar (the extensive country where the people dress in white) and rGya-nag (the extensive country where the people dress in black), respectively. In respect of Lahul there is known no such peculiar practice of wearing white cap so that they may be distinguished as 'white cap wearers.' The construction of the term as dkar-zhva also does not conform to the principles of grammar of the language according to which it should have been zhva-dkar. As such the suggestions appear to be merely speculative.

On this analogy some other scholars write it as Gar-zhva giving the name a Tibetan literary form which term then means 'dancing cap.' By all means this term also is inappropriate.

**Gar-zha in Tibetan Literature**

The Tibetan literature appears not to be familiar with the term Gar-zha. A well known Tibetan historical work deb-ther sngon-po (Blue Annals) gives two names as Ka-sha and Kha-sha similar to Gar-zha in a list of countries. But we cannot be sure if any of them refers to Lahul.

A work related to Padmasambhava possesses name of a country as Gha-sha among the list of a few great countries. Evans-Wentz writes, 'Padma preached to men in many parts of human world – in China, Assam, Gha-sha, …' In the note the Translator writes, 'or Ghar-sha (Gharsha khado gling), the country of dakinis, the present Lahoul, above Kulu,' (Evans-Wentz, 1954: 173). Here the form of the name used as Ghar-sha or Gha-sha are unusual. Moreover it is unlikely to see an unknown small territory placed in the class of such a big countries.

In a class of Tibetan literature composed by the Tibetan lama pilgrims who actually visited Lahul and have first hand knowledge of Lahul write Gar-sha for Lahul, instead of Gar-zha.

Gozang-pa (1189-1258) was the first siddha pilgrim from Tibet visiting Lahul. He stayed here for some period. In one of his two Namthars, itineraries, it is written as Gar-sha for Lahul, (rGod-tshang-a, 1974:132). sTag Tshang Ras-pa (1574-1651) was another Tibetan Teacher who visited Lahul and he stayed here for more than a year. He writes in his Namthar, Gar-sha for Lahul, (Ah, 6a.). Rang Rig Ras-pa (1595-1683) from Spiti and Nawang Tshering (1657-1730) from Zanskar, belonging to the neighbouring countries of Lahul, being familiar with the local traditions, both write Gar-zha for Lahul.

Azevedo, a European missionary who came from Guge through Ladakh in 1631, writes Carja and Caria for Lahul, (Wessels, 1924:113).. The traveller appears to transcribe the name Gar-zha in both the words. This he learnt at Darcha, at the head of Bhaga valley, the first village while entering Lahul from the side of Ladakh.

Jaschke in his Dictionary writes Gar-zha for Lahul. The two local works, 'Guide Books' (gNas-yig), for the holy places of Drilbu Ri (Gandhala) and Rephag (Triloknath) in Lahul write Gar-zha for Lahul, (i. gNas-yig of Dril-bu-Ri and Gandhola' (p.3a, L-3) and gNas-yig of Ras-'phags 'Phags-pa (p. 4b, L-4). Before Independence this term was the most popular in use because Lahulis had trade relations with Tibet. Rin-chhen bZang-po (958-1055), the great Translator, who in C.E. 975 went to Kashmir through Lahul writes Gar-zha for Lahul. This is the earliest reference and it is in the same form as we speak and write today.

**III. Lahul**

The name Lahul, the earliest is found mentioned in the work of the great Chinese scholar traveler Hiuen Tsiang in about C.E. 645. He writes, "Going north from this [Kullu], along a road, thick with dangers and precipices about 1800 to 1900 li along mountains and valleys, we come to the country of Lo-u-lo," (Beal, 1884, IV-177). Scholars like Cunningham, Francke, etc. all agree that it stands for Lahul. Presently the term Lahul is the most widely used name, among all the three.

**Lho-yul:** Alexander Cunningham suggests the term Lahul having originated from the Tibetan Lho-yul (the southern district), and this is the corrupt form of it. In his view this name was first given by the Ladakis to denote their southern district (Lho-yul = the southern country, province), (Cunningham, 1854: 24). Francke does not appear to agree with the suggestion. In this respect he writes that, "I cannot believe that Lahul is the Indian equivalent of a Tibetan word Lho-yul, 'south-land,' for I have never yet heard a Tibetan speaking of Lahul as Lho-yul. The name Lahul is used only by the people of Kulu," (Francke, 1908: 189).

We find no instance, in its history, of use of the term in Ladakh in this form for Lahul. Ladakh, both in written and in practice uses the term Garzha. None of the historians of Ladakh like Francke, Petech, Gergan, Tashi Rabgias, etc. are found to use this term. Rahul Sankrityayan similarly means by it the country of gods (Lha-yul). In this manner another meaning of the word could be suggested as the 'Country of Passes' (La-yul). These are, however, mere suggestions.

The geographical region of Lahul is found mentioned earliest in the Pali literature at several places by the expression as 'Chandrabhaga nadi tire,' i.e. on the 'banks of river Chandrabhaga' i.e. 'the valley of Chandrabhaga,' (Tobdan, 2022:101-152).

After Hiuen Tsiang this name is found in an inscription obtained from Lahul, in Sharda script and Sanskrit language. The inscription was read by Diwakar Nath Acharya who dates it to the period of early ninth century C.E. The ancient form of the name Lahul is given as Lāhuṇa.

In tradition the two neighbouring provinces of Pangi and Kullu, lying on the southern and western directions, have been addressing Lahul, in colloquy, by this name. The inhabitants of Kullu call it Lā-uḷa and those of Pangi as Lohal or Lauhal. P.K. Mattoo writes, in the context of Pangi, Lauhal for Lahul, (Mattoo, 1961:92). The visitors coming from the two directions call it similarly. In the medieval period in the work of Abhinava Gupta of Kashmir, in the Tantrik Sanskrit tradition, of the period tenth-eleventh century C.E., it writes Lāhulā for Lahul. Similarly in the Himachal folk traditions also it is found written as Lāhulā, (Tobdan, 2021: 151, 153). Thus this form of the name as 'Lahul' has been in constant use till the modern times in one of the two halves of the universe of Lahul.

Presently it is also the official name. The name was adopted for this purpose in the British period. It was then also used by the numerous scholars and travellers, mostly European. Then in the use of this name there are found variations in the spelling. One of the reasons is that writers came into contact with a similar word found in Persian as Lahaul. They took the two words Lahul and Lahaul as the same. There the word in the lexicons is given to mean as contempt, indifference, etc. Andrew Wilson suggests, writing the term with the spelling as 'Lahaul,' that, "Lahaul is a Hindustani word signifying a wilderness. It would not be far wrong to render it as a howling wilderness," (Wilson, 1876: 266).

This trend started after the middle of nineteenth century. It is thus found written in two more forms or with different spellings as: Lahaul and Lahoul. They are pronounced similarly.

The trend entered in the official use also. In the official works two forms of the name with the spellings as Lahul and Lahaul are found used.

The third form Lahoul is found used initially briefly then it remained in use only with the scholars. One set of government departments uses the name Lahul while the other set uses the name with the spelling as Lahaul. In their use they are consistent. They use the same form constantly without changing. The tradition started before the Independence and the same is being maintained even today scrupulously.

a. **Lahaul:** This term Lahaul was adopted in the official use perhaps for the first time in the list of the territories declared as 'Excluded Areas and Partialy Excluded Areas' under the Government of India Act, 1935. Thereafter it continued to be used in the Legal documents and Acts of the Laws. Thus we find the name in the form as Lahaul in use in the subsequent documents as under;

   i. The Spiti and Lahaul Laws Regulation, 1942 (Punjab Regulation No. 1 of 1942).

   ii. The Constitution of India of the Independent India in the expression as 'The Constitution Sheduled Tribes Order 1950, C.O. 22, Part XIII, Himachal Pradesh.'

   iii. The Punjab Reorganisation Act, 1966 (31 of 1966), and

   iv. The State of Himachal Pradesh Act, 1970 (Act No. 53 of 1970).

   In the Summary Settlement Report of 1855 of district Kangra, of which Lahul formed a part, prepared by George Carnac Barnes the name is used in the form as 'Lahoul' (para. 392). In the Regular Settlement Report of 1876 of district Kangra by James B. Lyall it is written with the changed spelling as 'Lahaul', (para. 129).

   Presently the practice of use of the name with the spelling as 'Lahaul' is found in the correspondences and documents of the district Administration of the district and the Election office.

b. **Lahul:** Some other offices follow the name with the spelling as 'Lahul,' the historical form of the name. The sets of departments using the term are the Gazetteers and documents of Census Department. In the Gazetteers we see the earliest application of the term Lahul in the first District Gazetteer, the Gazetteer of District Kangra of 1897. Thereafter we see in the Imperial Gazetteer of India where it is written with diacritical marks as Lāhul, (Imperial Gazetteer, 1909: 165). This tradition under the Gazetteers has been carried on in the modern times. In the latest edition of the District Gazetteer of district

Lahul-Spiti of 1972 it writes 'Lahul.' In the case of Census also, the District Census Handbook 2011 it is spelt as Lahul.

All the three forms of the name are found used by the writers of the British period. Alexander Cunningham, (1854), A.H. Francke (1926), and J. Hutchison & J.Ph. Vogel (1933) write Lahul in their works. Moorcroft (1841), A.F.P. Harcourt (1871), C.G. Bruce (1914), Walter Asboe (1946), etc., write Lahoul.

Among the modern writers O.C. Handa and Tulsi Raman, the most commonly known writers of the State on the subject, write 'Lahul.' The H.P. Language, Culture and Art Academy also uses the term 'Lahul.' Among the local writers of Lahul, District Lahul-Spiti, C. Dorje and Balram write Lahul. Ram Nath Sahni writes Lahoul. Tobdan since his first publication in 1984 has been using the word with the spelling as 'Lahul. Historically 'Lāhul' is the oldest form of the name.

McArthur, of a University in London, who had worked in the Survey of India, before the Independence of India, made a mountaineering expedition and survey work with a team from the Survey of India, in 1955, in the high Central Lahul, where perhaps few Lahulis might have reached. He discusses and examines in his article the different forms of the name 'Lahul,' looking at it in practice and history. He finds that the most appropriate name is with the spelling of 'Lahul.' He also confirms that it is written 'Lahul' in the Survey of India Sheet 52H, (McArthur, 1956: 289). Tobdan has discussed these names, (Tobdan, 1973).

**People's Geography of Lahul**

Geographically Lahul consists of three valleys: Chandra, Bhaga and the combined valley of Chandrabhaga. Culturally this is broadly divided into four divisions: Tinan consisting of the whole Chandra valley; sTod, the upper part of Bhaga valley; Gahar, the lower part of Bhaga valley; and Pattan, the Chandrabhaga valley. These also remained the political divisions immediately before the British period. Tinan was ruled by the thakurs of Gundhla, sTod by the thakurs of Khangsar also known as Kolong; Gahar by that of Gungrang; and Pattan was directly under the raja of Kullu. The area below Thirot was known as Chamba-Lahul and was under the rajas of Chamba.

The four major geographical-cultural divisions are also the linguistic divisions. Thus the Linguistic geography of Lahul may be given as: sTodpa in sTod, Gahari in Gahar, Tinani in Tinan and Pattani in Pattan. In Tinan valley around Khoksar the language is dialect of Bhoti. In Miyar valley the area close to Udaipur speaks Pattani and the upper part Miyari, a dialect of Bhoti. The area around Tindi, border with Pangi, speaks Pangwali. There are two other languages named Chinali or Shipi (Shibi) and Lohari or mGar-ra. sTodpa is a dialect of Bhoti. The languages of Chinal and Lohari are of the class of Indo-Aryan. The other three are quite different from each other and may be placed in one separate class. Grierson classifies them under Tibeto-Burman, Pronominalised.

Below are given names of different places as they are spoken by the people of different areas of Lahul:

| **Name of the Place, etc.** | **The term by which the place, etc. is known in the language of** | | | |
|---|---|---|---|---|
| **Item/Language** | **Pattani** | **Tinani** | **Gāharī** | **Todpā** |
| Kullu - area | Ramdī | Ramdī | Kuzu | Nyungti |
| Kullu – Town | Sārang | Sārang | Gyalsa | Gyalsa |
| Inhabitants of Kullu | Kuza | Kuza | Kuza | Mon |
| Manali (when it was not yet developed to town) | Daṇa | Daṇa | Daṇa | Daṇa |
| Lahul | Songlā | Garzha | Garzha | Garzha |
| sTod | sTod | sTod | sTod | sTod |
| Pattan | Chāngsā | Chāngsā | Melogs | Manchhad |
| Gāhar | Gāhar | Gāhar | -- | Punan |
| Tinan | Tinan | Tinan | Tinan | Tinan |
| Miyāḷ Nala | Miyāḷ | Miyāḷ | Miyāḷ | Patanam |

Here in the first column downwards are given the names of the items or particulars. Then towards the right are given the item as it is spoken in the particular language. Thus the region of Kullu in Pattani is called Ramdi and the Kullu town, as it was the capital, as Sārang

The residents of the four areas of Lahul are known as Manchhadpa, Punanpa, Tinanpa and sTodpa in sTodpa language; Changspa, Tinanpa, sTodpa in Gahari; and Changspa, Tinanba, Gahari, sTodpa in Tinani and

Pattani. The people of the areas beyond Kullu are known in sTodpa as mTha'-pa (of the distant land), and as Pardeshi (of other land) in Pattani.

The valleys of Chandra and Chandrabhaga are further subdivided into smaller divisions which may be given as under:

**Chandrabhaga Valley**

**Logsā:** The area between Mūling or Tandī and Kīrting or as some others say between Mooling and Loppā.

| | | |
|---|---|---|
| Changsā | = | From Kirting down to Yombe; or Logadd i.e. Lote Nala to Yombe (Junda) |
| Gūnam or Gūnambar | = | Thirot to Udaipur, or from Dhudhgadh (Junda Nala) to Thirot |
| Reupa, Rebag | = | Thirot to Udaipur |
| Mamba | = | Udaipur to Madgran |
| Miyar Nala or Patanam | = | Miyar Nala, the valley of the stream falling in Udaipur |
| Tsokhang Gār | = | Thirot Nala |
| **Tinan valley:** | | |
| Tinan | = | Dālāng to Shūling |
| Ranglo | = | Ropsang to Teling |
| Khoksar | = | Teling to Khoksar |
| Ya-ri Khoksar | = | Old Khoksar |

Many villages in Lahul possess more than one name as given below:

| Common name | Additional name |
|---|---|
| Pyukar | Chugṭā |
| Stingrī | Tingrig |
| Kyelang | Kelāng |
| Guśāl | Gudung, Gus, Guī , Kuluta |
| Tandī | Tāngtī |
| Ṭholong | Chhod |

| | |
|---|---|
| Loṭ | Loppe, Lod |
| Jāhlmā | Yambe, Yanaphel |
| Śānaśā | Ṣāngme, Śāng |
| Goram | Gormā |
| Lindūr | Ling-tog, Ling-stod, |
| Othang | Au-tamar |
| Ḍhwānśā | Ḍabayi |
| Junḍā | Yombe |
| Nālḍā | Nal Lang |
| Kiśorī | Khering |
| Chhagtsalgang | A place near Triloknath. |
| Hinsā | Menzang |
| Triloknath | Tunde, Rebag |
| Udaipur | Margul, Maru |
| Madgrāṅ | Mādūṅgā |
| Gundhlā | Tinan, Gule |
| Gandhala | Gandhola |
| Tubchiling | Tukiling |

Gundhla is in Tinan valley, Pyukar, Stingri and Kyelang are in Gahar. All other villages fall in Pattan valley. The names mChhod, Lod, Yanaphel, Shang, Khering, Menzang and Chugta are used only by the sTodpas.

Rebagpas call the people of the upper areas in Pattan as Philogpa. The upper part of Pattan is called Lhogsa (Lho-sa) and the middle as Changsa (byang-sa). Literally the first term means Southern Land and the second term means Northern Land. Manchhad is spelt as sMan-chhad and Melogs as sMad-logs.

# 12

## Lahul: A Historical Sketch

Lahul lies between the Mid Himalaya or Pir Panjal range and the Western Himalaya or Baralacha range. Its inhabited part is situated at the average height of about 9000 feet above the sea level. In the Census of 2011 there were 19,107 souls living in Lahul.

Lahul is a part, forming one of the two sub-divisions, of district Lahul-Spiti, in the state of Himalachal Pradesh. Lahul-Spiti was formed into a district in 1966. Before this it was a sub-division of tehsil Kullu in district Kangra, in the state of Panjab. It was merged with the Himachal Pradesh state in 1970 after the reorganization of Panjab. In 1975 the part of Lahul, known as Chamba-Lahul, constituting 118 villages, in four patwar circles, which earlier was under the Chamba state forming part of Pangi, in district Chamba, was merged with Lahul.

Lahul is known by three names as Lahul, Garzha and Songla. Hiuen Tsiang, a great scholar and traveller, from China, came to India in search of Buddhist scriptures. In the Western Himalaya he reached in c. C.E. 645 into the most interior point upto K'iu-lu-to, i.e. Ku-lu-ta, the modern Kullu. From here, Kuluta, HiuenTsiang makes observation of the countries lying beyond in the northern direction and writes, 'Going north from this, along a road thick with dangers and precipices, along mountains and valleys, we come to the country of Lo-u-lo,' (Lahul). He describes Lahul as the first country immediately beyond Kullu. Scholars have no doubt that it indicates to Lahul of the present. This name Lahul is found inscribed in an inscription, obtained from Lahul, written in Sharda script and Sanskrit language. The inscription was read by Diwakar Nath Acharya. He writes that the script used here retains some features of the Gupta script. So he calls it proto-Sharda and gives date around the ninth century. The ancient form of the name Lahul given here is as Lā-hu-ṇa. The name Lahul is practically not used by the inhabitants of Lahul. It is used in slightly changed form by the natives of Kullu and Pangi, and by all those coming from those sides and speaking similar languages.

The name Gar-zha is used by the inhabitants of the valleys of Chandra and Bhaga. It is also used by the people living in the regions on its northern side like Zanskar, Ladak and Spiti. It is also used in Tibetan literature but there it is found slightly varying. The earliest evidence of its use is found in C.E. 975, in the Namthar, itinirary, of Rinchhen Zangpo, exactly in the form as we write and use today. It is used with two epithets as Gar-zha Kha-'dro gLing i.e. Lahul the land of Dakinis and Gar-zha Ral-gSum i.e. Lahul having three manes, having three mountain ranges. The name Songla (Songlā) is used by a section of people in Lahul, the inhabitants of Pattan valley.

Geographically it constitutes the valleys of Chandra, Bhaga and some portion of the valley of the river Chandrabhaga upto Rohli which runs north-east to south-west. It is bounded on the south by Bara Bhanghal of the Kangra district and by Kullu; on the east by Spiti; on the north by Zanskar and Ladakh; and on the west by Pangi and Bharmaur.

Lahul constituted a buffer between the two great international Cultural zones. On its north lies that of Central Asian and on the south Indo-Aryan. A long route which formed part of the great International Silk Route, existing from the ancient times, linked the two great cultural and economic zones. It passed through Lahul crossing the regions of Kullu, Lahul, Ladakh, etc. This route connected the fertile and productive plains of the north and north-west India with the silk producing rich markets of Central Asia like Yarkand, Kashgar, etc.

There exist four distinct cultures which are divided on the basis of geography and language. These are: sTod, Punan, Tinan and Manchhad or Pattan. It also has other linguistic-social classes. It was divided politically in the same manner. During the period of pre-Independence the regional chiefs constituted: the Thakurs of Khangsar, also known as Kolong to the outsiders, the chiefs of sTod; of Gungrang, the chiefs of Punan; and the Thakurs of Gundhla, the chiefs of Tinan i.e. Chandra valley. These were suzerains of the raja of Kullu. Pattan was directly ruled by the rajas of Kullu. A portion of Lahul named Chamba-Lahul, below Thirot, was under the rule of Chamba state. It is not known if Lahul ever remained under one local ruler.

Religiously it follows Buddhism and Hinduism. They all practice folk religion which is much varied. Different deities are propitiated in different areas, even villages, on different occasions. There are small temples dedicated to some deities but they are not known at any other place. Gepang with eight other associated deities is the chief deity of whole Lahul. It has its principal temple at Yangling just above Khwagling i.e. Sissu, and the present functional temple is situated at Srasrin, Shashin. It is situated on the other side of the nallah towards Tandi.

At Mayling, in Pattan, there is a damaged statue of Shiva with three figures carved on stone. People call it Mahadeva. It is kept aside in the compound. There are also some carved wooden pieces which might have formed part of a fallen temple. Specialists date the statue to about 9th century C.E. and link it with Kashmir art. At the place there is a small temple where the villagers worship *lingas* placed there. Margul is Hindu temple. It has in the ceiling carvings on wood panels of the Buddha and scenes related to his life.

Indian Buddhism reached here quite early. There are several monuments still standing witness to the fact. There are carvings of the Bodhisattvas done on rocks lying on the waysides in the valleys of Chandra and Bhaga which formed a part of the ancient silk route, passed through Kullu, Lahul, Ladakh, etc.

During the reign of the emperor Asoka, after the conclusion of the third Buddhist Council under the aegis of emperor Asoka, c. 250 B..C.E., a team of five theras headed by Majjhima was sent to the Himalayas to work in the border countries for the propagation of the Dhamma. They met Mahakappina, the king of Kukkuta or Kuluta, modern Kullu. The raja as a result of discourses of the theras, enterned the path of the Doctrine. His men followed him. Then the raja, his men and the missionaries, moved to the banks of river Chandrabhaga, Lahul. They recognised the inhabitants of the area as Kinnara and subjugated them to the following of the Dhamma. They surveyed the region and named the rivers, the main river and its two heads, the mountains, etc. They worked much for the Dhamma there and founded monuments. Gandhala may be considered as the principal among them as it is situated at a prominent place, at the mountain tip at the confluence of the river Chandra and Bhaga. There were found some archaeological artifacts here. Scholars date it earliest to 1$^{st}$ century B.C.E. The place is located in the middle of Lahul. They made it a place of pilgrimage. There are verses written by the theras and theris found in the collections in the famous Pali works like Theragatha, Therigatha, Apadana, Atthakatha of Dhammapala, etc. They write that they in their previous life in the life of Kinnara lived on the banks of Chandrabhaga. The place might have been a famous place of pilgrimage and there might have been coming many pilgrims. The learned theras and theris made the place famous in the Pali literature as 'the Banks of river Chandrabhaga.' This name makes the area easily recognisable even if the name of the place is lost or changed to some other name in the long history. It is possible that they gave name to the country also.

The earliest mention of the place in the Pali literature is found in the jataka named Chanda-Kinnara jataka. The Buddha and Yashodhara, in one of their earlier life as Boddhisattva, in the life of Kinnara, lived on the mount named Chanda which has been identified with Gandhala. Among the monuments related to Indian Buddhism, earliest is the monastery of Gandhala where a lotah, vase, of mixed metal was discovered. Earlier it was dated by Charles Horne as c. C.E. 200-300. It has now been re-examined and has been pre-dated to 1st century B.C.E. The object was collected by major Hay who came here personally when he was posted as Assistant Commissioner at Kullu of which Lahul formed a part. The local people had taken away some other valuable objects but the lotah was saved due to the wisdom and promptness of the Officer. This is an object of importance of history not only of Lahul but of the whole country. Some other monuments like the Gundhla castle and the Khangsar mKhar are lying today unattended. There was also found a head of Bodhisattva of marble which was lost to thieves. The Triloknath temple is the standing monument where there is an inscription indicating to its foundation. At Chhokhor, near Sissu, the objects of worship in the monastery are all of Indian Buddhism. There are carvings on rocks of the Bodhisattvas at Gundhla, Kyelang, Kardang and Srangbar (Khangsar). There was also one in the Pattan valley which was broken up during the construction of the road. These belong to Indian Buddhism. There is also a carving on rock of the Buddha, called as Child Buddha, at Kolong.

Rinchhen Zangpo (958-1055), the Great Translator, while going for studying Sanskrit and Buddhism, to Kashmir in C.E. 975. came through Piti and Khunu, i.e. Spiti and Kinnaaur, and passed through Lahul, which he writes as Garzha. There are two monasteries accredited to Rinchhen Zangpo: Zho-ling and Gungrang. Of the two wooden images found in

Zholing one is in England in a museum and the other is in the Himachal Pradesh State Museum at Shimla. The two monasteries are now deserted. Thus Tibetan Buddhism firmly came in the time of Rinchhen Zangpo.

There may have come many pilgrim siddhas from Tibet from time to time. We have information available about some of the renowned Siddha Lamas who went on pilgrimage through Lahul to Jalandhara i.e. Kangra, and Uddiyana, in the Swat valley, now in Pakistan. Uddiyana or Urgyan is considered as the birth place of guru Padmasambhava. These pilgrims stayed in Lahul each for more than a year. Gozangpa (rGyal-ba rGod-tshang-pa, 1189-1258) is the first siddha about whom we have information of his visit to Lahul. Thereafter came his disciple Urgyanpa (Urgyan Seng-ge dPal, 1230-1309). He was first to visit Urgyan and is famous as Urgyanpa. There is an image of Urgyanpa, with a typical cap indicative of symbol of Urgyan, in the monastery at Chhukutsi, Khangsar. sTagTshang Raspa (Ngag-dbang rGya-mtsho, 1574-1651) came to be called as the Second Urgyanpa. Only Urgyanpa and sTag-tshang Raspa could complete their pilgrimage to Urgyan. Therefor the two are famous as Urgyanpa. sTag-tshang Raspa visited Uddiyana under the most difficult conditions, nearly impossible. But his determination was unshakable. He went twice in 1613, when he had to drop the journey halfway, and then in 1615. He completed the journey the next time which he did mostly alone. Nawang (NGag-dbang) Tshe-ring (1657-1730) from Zanskar and Rang-rig Ras-pa (1595-1683) from Spiti also stayed in Lahul for long time. Nawang Tshering founded the monastery at Yobrang. These lamas stayed in Lahul for more than a year while they were on journey to other places. Lahul was fascinating for them for several reasons. It was geographically congenial. Socially they had no problem. It was mostly Buddhist and there were several ancient Buddhist monuments and sites for visit.

Tashi Tamphel (bKra-shis sTan-'phel, 1820-1890) came from Ladakh. He was a lama of Hemis and sTagna, later Rinpochhe. He was a scholar and artist, like painter, carver, etc. He stayed in Lahul for several years between c. 1880-1890 and worked in several monasteries like Gandhala, Tayul, Gemur, etc. There he renovated the monasteries, did the work of carving, painting, etc.

Monasteries related to Tibetan Buddhism are at Gemur, Shashur, Labrang, Kardang, Khoksar, Silla, Chhokhor, Beeling, Othang, Chhukutsi, etc. There are gnas-bshad, guidebooks, regarding Gandhala-Drilbu Ri and

Rebag-Triloknath. As the prevalence of Indian Buddhism got weakened in the area, Tibetan Buddhism took over the practice. It kept the practice of Buddhism live in Lahul after it disappeared at other places.

Lahul, alongwith Kullu, was taken over by the British rule, in 1846. Before this it remained under the Sikhs for a brief period. Before this it was under Kullu. Moorcroft came in 1820 and passed through Lahul. He met thakur Dharm Singh of Khangsar. Cunningham came twice, once in 1839, for the survey work. Thereafter there came many European writer-travellers who wrote about Lahul.

Moravian missionaries opened their office in around 1854. Initially they settled at Kardang then they shifted to Kyelang. Jaescke of the mission came in around 1857 and remained here for about three years. He wrote a grammar on Tibetan language and the Tibetan English dictionary. A.H. Francke remained at Kyelang for about two years between 1906 and 1908. He worked intensively in search of the documents of historical importance. These are contained in his two works named First and Second 'Collection of Tibetan Historical Inscriptions on Rock and Stone from Western Tibet.' These have been published in original in the work entitled 'Moravian Missionaries in Western Trans-Himalaya' (2008). The transcription in Roman and translation are given in 'Historical Documents from Western Trans-Himalaya Lahul, Zanskar and Ladakh' (1996). Both the works are authored by Tobdan and C. Dorje. Some other missionaries like Asboe also wrote on Lahul. Asboe has about four or five articles on Lahul. They also wrote a chapter from the Bible in the three languages of Lahul. The most renowned of the missionaries who lived at Kyelang for the longest period, nearly fifty years, is Mr. Heyde.

Rohtang Atal Tunnel was inaugurated by the Prime Minister in October, 2020. It has become beneficial to the people of Ladakh, Lahul and Pangi and also is an object of attraction for the tourists. The travel through the Rohtang pass is now mostly done by the tourists for joy.

# 13

# Bird's Eye View of the Geography of the Himalaya

Grierson, taking the central and western divisions of the Himalaya as geographically one unit, gave one collective name to the languages of the whole region as Pahari. He took this name as it was current in practice in his time. We don't go into the origin of the term and its significance here. Also we have not been able to take into account a good part of the Himalaya, its eastern division. After the independence Nepal adopted the name Nepali, based on the name of the majority population and its language, to name its major language and bring all the other small languages under this name, dropping the term Pahari. Similarly Uttrakhand gave names as Kumaoni and Garhwali to its languages.

On the other hand Himachal Pradesh remained undecided in this regard. Himachal also did not have such opportunity. There does not appear to have been any effort also in this direction. Its effort appears to be to obtain constitutional recognition to the name. We are, however, not aware of its proper form and relevance in the changed circumstances. The linguistic picture of Himachal is slightly different from those of Nepal and Uttrakhand. Here the number of languages is more. There are nearly fifty or so number of languages here. They are all well developed and living, although some of them are on the decline. These languages also belong to different linguistic families. The valuable asset bothers none.

In the formation of the linguistic map of the whole Himalaya there appears a good deal of role played by the physical geography of the region during the course of its long history. Nepal and Uttrakhand, which form the central division of the Himalaya, have many languages but there are a few languages which have large number of speakers so they have named their languages as such. This part of the Himalaya rises slowly from its base from the plains and reaches the un-habitable parts of the heights. The spread of the land is comparatively easy and less in breadth. The regions being comparatively accessible was favourable for the growth of larger communities with developed homogenous cultures and languages. It was thus also congenial for the states to grow larger in size.

The western Himalaya, comprising the present state of Himachal Pradesh, stretches long through the river valleys, between the plains and the high Himalayan ranges. It was more difficult for approach and communication within. The populations in the history remained less disturbed except at the border regions. There exist a number of small cultural groups and linguistic pockets.

This stretch of western Himalaya first extends from the plains to the range of the Outer Himalaya or Dhauladhar range, then to mid Himalaya or the Pir Panjal range and lastly to the Western Himalaya or the Greater Himalaya.

In the higher western Himalaya, Lahul lies between the Mid Himalaya and the Western or the Greater Himalaya, or between the Pir Panjal range and Baralacha or Zanskar range. This part of the area extending from the valleys of the headwaters of the river Chandrabhaga towards the east and covering the valleys of headwaters of Satluj constituted the ancient Kimpurushavarsh or Kinnarland. The geography of the Himalaya in the time of Asoka was fully known. Asoka sent teams of missionaries to the regions of the headwaters of Chandrabhaga and Satluj i.e. Suvarnabhumi, the modern Guge, fully covering the border countries of the Himalaya.

# Bibliography

**Books in English**

Agrawal, V.S. 1963. Matsya Purana, A Study, All India Kashiraj Trust, Varanasi.

Ali, S.M. 1966. Geography of the Puranas, People's Publishing House, New Delhi.

Atkinson, T Edwin. 1981. The Himalayan Districts of North-estern Provinces, vol. I-II, Allahabad. Cosmo, New Delhi, reprint. `

Bamzai, P.N.K. 1994. Cultural and Political History of Kashmir, vols. 1 to 3, M.D., New Delhi.

Barnes, George Carnac. 1852. Report on the Settlement on the District of Kangra in the Trans-Satluj States, Lahore. Para. 392.

Basham, A.L. 1954. The Wonder That was India, Grove Press, New York, 1959.

Beal, Samuel, (Tr.). 1884. Si-yu-ki, Buddhist Records of the Western World, vol. I & II. Translated from the Chinese of Hiuen Tsiang, reprinted 1969, Munshiram Manoharlal, Delhi.

Beotra, B.R. 1924. A Gazetteer of the Suket State, Calcutta.

Bhattacharya, B. 1968. The Indian Buddhist Iconography, Firma K.L. Mukhopadhyaya, Calcutta.

Bruce, C.G. 1914. Kulu and Lahoul, Edward Arnold, London.

Census of India, 2011. Himachal Pradesh, Part XII-B, District Census Handbook Lahul & Spiti.

Chakladar, H.C. 1925. The Geography of Kalidas, Indian Studies, Calcutta.

Chatterji, Suniti Kumar. 1974. Kirata-Jana-Krti, The Indo-Mongoloids, Their Contributions to the History and Culture of India, The Asiatic Society of Bengal, Calcutta, reprinted.

Chattopadhyaya, Debiprasad (Ed.). 1970. Taranatha's History of Buddhism in India, Motilal Banarsidass, Delhi, translated by Lama Chimpa and Alaka Chattopadhayaya, reprinted 1990.

Cleghorn, H. 1864. Report upon the Forests of the Punjab and the Western Himalaya, Roorkee.

Colin Rosser. 1956. The Political System of a Himalayan Community, Dessertation presented for the Degree of Ph. D. in Anthropology in the University of London, (School of Oriental and African Studies) [Unpublished].

Coomarsawamy, A.K. 1931, Yaksas, Parts I and II, reprinted, Munshiram Manoharlal, New Delhi..

Cowell, E.B. 1895-1907. The Jataka or Stories of the Buddha's Former Births, Set I & II, Low Price Publications, Delhi, reprinted 1993.

Cunningham, Alexander. 1854. Ladak, Physical, Statistical and Historical, reprinted, 1970, Sagar, New Delhi.

Cunningham, Alexander. 1879. The Stupa of Bharhut, A Buddhist Monument, W.H. Allen, London.

Cunningham, Alexander. 1891. Coins of Ancient India, London.

Cunningham, Alexander. 1924. The Ancient Geography of India, Munshiram Manoharlal, New Delhi, reprinted 2002.

Davids, Mrs. Rhys. 1909. Psalms of the Early Buddhists, I.- Psalms of the Sisters, Pali Text Society, London.

Davids Mrs. Rhys. 1913. Psalms of the Early Buddhists, Vol. II.- Psalms of the Brethren, Pali Text Society, London.

Diack, A.H. 1896. The Kulu Dialect of Hindi.

Dowson, John. 1888. A Classical Dictionary of Hindu Mythology and Religion.

Errington, Elizabeth & Joe Cribb (Ed.). 2012. Vase with Incised Scenes, The Ancient Indie & Iran Trust, Cambridge. The Crossroads of Asia: Transformation in Image & Symbol, pp. 163-164.

Evans-Wentz, W.Y. 1954. The Tibetan Book of the Great Liberation, Oxford, London.

Francke, A.H. 1907. A History of Western Tibet, reprinted, 1995, Asian Educational Services, New Delhi.

Gazetteer. 1897. Gazetteer of the Kangra District, Parts II to IV, Kullu, Lahul and Spiti 1897. Indus, New Delhi, reprinted.

Gazetteer. 1904. Chamba State.

Gazetteer. 1917. Punjab District Gazetteer. Vol. XXX A, Kangra District, Parts II, III and IV, Lahore.

Gazetteer of Kashmir and Ladak. 1890.

Gazetteer Imperial. 1909. Imperial Gazetteer of India. 1909. New Series, vol. 16, Oxford.

Geiger, Wilhelm. 1912. The Mahavamsa, Pali Text Society, London.

Getty, Alice. 1928. The Gods of Northern Buddhism, Oxford.

Goetz, Hermann. 1955. The Early Wooden Temples of Chamba, Brill, Leiden.

Gore, F. St. J. 1895. The Light and Shades of Hill Life, Kulu, Kuram. London.

Government of India Act, 1935, The Schedule.

Government of India, The Constitution of India.

Grierson, G.A. 1908. Linguistic Survey of India, Vol. III, Tibeto-Burman Family, Part I. Motilal Banarsidass, Delhi. reprinted 1967.

Harcourt, A. Captain. 1870. Rambles in Kooloo, Pioneer Press, Allahabad.

Harcourt, A.F.P. 1871. The Himalayan Districts of Kooloo, Lahoul & Spiti, William H. Allen & Co., London, reprinted Vivek Publishing House, Delhi, 1972.

Hermanns, Mathias. 1954. The Indo-Tibetans, The Indo-Tibetans and Mongloid Problem and the Southern Himalaya and North-North-east India, K.L. Fernandes, Bombay.

Himachal Pradesh District Gazetteers. 1972. Lahul & Spiti, 1972.

Hutchison, J. 1923. Guide to Dalhousie, Chamba and the Inner Mountains between Simla and Kashmir.

Hutchison, J. and Vogel, J. Ph. 1933. History of the Panjab Hill States, Part II, Lahore. Reprinted Department of Languages and Culture, H.P. Shimla, 1982.

Kale, M.R. 1924. A Literal Translation of Bana's Kadambari (Purvabhaga complete), Vaman Yashwant & Co., Bombay.

Kirkpatrick, Colonel. 1811. An Account of the Kingdom of Nepaul, reprinted Manjusri, New Delhi, 1969.

Lakshman Sarup. 1967. The Nighantu and the Nirukta, the oldest Indian treatises on Etymology, Philology and Semantics, (English Translation), Motilal Banarsidas, Delhi.

Law, B.C. 1933. The History of Pali Literature, Vol. I, Kegan Paul, London.

Law, B.C. 1943. Tribes in Ancient India, Poona.

Lyall, J.B. 1876. Final Report on the Revised Settlement of Kangra District. Para. 129.

Mahinda, Samner (Anagarika Mahendra). 2020. Theragathapali, Book of Verses of Bhikhus, Dhamma Publishers, Roslindale, MA, USA.

Malalsekera, G.P. 1937. Dictionary of Pali Proper Names, Vol. I, John Murray, London.

Malalasekera, G.P. 1938. Dictionary of Pali Proper Names, Vol. II, John Murray, London.

Mankad, D.R. 1951. Puranic Chronology, Gangajala, Ananda.

Mattoo, P.K. 1961. Report on the changing pattern of Administration on the people of Pangi, in Pal Singh, Village Survey.

McCrindle, J. W. 1901. Ancient India as Described in Classical Literature, Eastern Book, Patna, reprinted 1987.

Menon, Ramesh. 2009. The Complete Mahabharata, Vol. 2, Rupa, New Delhi.

Mitra, A. 1953. Tribes and Castes of West Bengal, Census 1951, West Bengal Government.

Minakshi Chaudhary. 1998. Exploring Pangi Himalaya, Indus, New Delhi.

Moti Chandra. 1945. Geographical and Economic Studies in the Mahabharata, Upayana Parva, U.P. Historical Society, Lucknow.

Oldenberg, H. 1879. The Dipavamsa, London.

Pal Singh, R.C. (Ed.). 1961. Village Survey Kupha, Parmas, Thamoh, Malet.

Panchmukhi, R.S. 1951. Gandharvas and Kinnaras in Indian Iconography, Kannada Research Institute, Dharwar.

Pandit, R.S. 1935. Rajatarangini, The Saga of the Kings of Kasmir, Sahitya Akademi, New Delhi, reprinted. 1977.

Pati Ram Bahadur. 1916. Garhwal, Ancient and Modern, Simla.

Petech, L. 1977. The Kingdom of Ladakh (c. 950–1842 AD), Instituto Italiano, Roma.

Punjab Govt. 1918. Ruling Princes and Cheifs, Notables and Principal Officials of the Punjab Native States, Punjab Govt., Lahore.

Punjab Reorganisation Act, 1966, (31 of 1966).

Quintanilla, S.R. 2007. History of Early Stone Sculpture at Mathura, c. 150 BCE-100 CE., Brill.

Rajputana District Gazetteers. 1904. Ajmer-Merwara, Vol. I-A, 1904.

Regmi, D.R. 1952. Ancient and Medieval Nepal, Kathmandu.

Risley, H.H. 1891. Tribes and Castes of Bengal, Vol. I. Calcutta.

Russel, R.V. 1916. The Tribes and Castes of the Central Provinces of India, Vol. III, Macmillan & Co., London.

Shukla, L.K. 1972. A Study of Hindu Art and Architecture, Chowkhamba, Varanasi.

Shukla, R.K. 2003. The Geography of the Ramayan, Koshal Book Depot, New Delhi.

Singh, G.P. 1990. The Kiratas in Ancient India, Gian, New Delhi,.

Smith, Gisborne. 1891. Report on the Pangi Leased Forests, Chamba State, with proposal for their management for 10 years, in Pal Singh, Village Survey, 1961.

Snellgrove, D.L. 1957. Buddhist Himalaya. Philosophical Library, New York.

Spiti and Lahaul Laws Regulation, 1942, (Punjab Regulation No. 1 of 1942).

State of Himachal Pradesh Act, 1970, (Act No. 53 of 1970).

Stein, M.A. 1900. Kalhana's Rajatarangini, A Chronicle of the Kings of Kashmir, Vol. I & II, Archibald Constable & Co., Westminster.

Taluqdar. 1916. The Matsya Purana, Sacred Books of Hindus, Vol. XVII, Part I, Allahabad.

Tobdan. 1984. History and Religions of Lahul, Books Today, New Delhi.

Tobdan. 1993. The People of the Upper Valley, the sTodpas of Lahul in the Himalaya, Book India, Delhi.

Tobdan. 2008. The Canda-Kinnara Jataka, and the Kinnara and the Canda Parvata, in Expressions in Indian Art (Essays in Memory of Sh. M.C. Joshi), 2008, Edited by B.R. Mani and Alok Tripathi, Agam Prakashan, New Delhi, (Vol. II: 459-464).

Tobdan. 2008a. Cultural History of Western trans-Himalayas – Bashahar-Kinnaur, Aryan Books International, New Delhi.

Tobdan. 2021a. Ancient Lahul and Himalaya, Kaveri Books, New Delhi.

Tobdan. 2021b. Exploring Malana, Kinnara Malana.

Tobdan. 2022. Ancient Lahul, The Kinnaraland in the Himalaya.

Tripathi, R.S. 1937. History of Kanauj to the Moslem Conquest, Motilal Banarsidass, Delhi

Upadhyaya, Bhagwatisaran. 1947. India in Kalidas, Kitabistan, Allahabad.

Ved Kumari. 1968. The Nilmat Purana (A Cultural and Literary Study of a Kasmiri Purana), Vol. I, J.K. University, Jammu (Tawi).

Viyogi, Naval. 2002. Nagas: The Ancient Rulers of India, Their Origin and History, Originals, New Delhi.

Vogel, J.Ph. 1909. Annual Report, Archaeological Survey of India, 1905-6.

Vogel, J. Ph. 1911. Antiquities of Chamba State, Part I, Archaeological Sruvey of India, New Delhi.

Walters, Jonathan S. 2018. The Legends of the Buddhist Saints - Apadanapali, Part –I, the Legends of the Theras, Jonathan S. Walters and Whitman College.

Walters, Jonathan S. 2018a. The Legends of the Buddhist Saints, - Apadanapali, Part II, The Legends of the Theris, Jonathan S. Walters and Whitman College.

Walton, H.G. 1910. British Garhwal, A Gazetteer, Vol. XXXVI.

Walton, H.G. 1911. Almora, A Gazeteer, Vol. XXXV.

Wessels, C. 1924. Early Jesuit Travellers in Central Asia, 1603-1721, The Hague, AES Reprint New Delhi, 1999.

William Pruitt (Tr.). 1998. The Commentaries on the Verses of Theris: (Therigatha), Atthakatha Paramatthadippani VI, by Acarya Dhammapala. Pali Text Society, Oxford 1999.

Wilson, Andrew. 1876. The Abode of Snow, William Blackwood, London.

Wright, Daniel. (1877). History of Nepal, Cambridge.

**Journals in English**

Buhler, G. 1892. The Two Prasastis of Baijnath, Epigraphia Indica, Vol. I, Archaeological Survey of India, New Delhi, reprinted 1983 (pp. 97-118).

Charles Horne. 1871. Notes on an Ancient Indian Vase, with an Account of the Engravings thereupon, The Journal of the Royal Asiatic Society of Great Britain and Ireland, New Series, Vol. 5, (367-375).

Das, S.R. 1954. A Note on Kinnaras. Man in India, March 1954, Vol. 34, pp. 40-46.

Francke, A.H. 1908. 'Note on Moloso' in the Journal of the Royal Asiatic Society of Great Britain and Ireland, for 1908.

Giusepee, Father. 1807. An Account of the Kingdom of Nepal, Asiatic Researches, Volume Second, Calcutta, pp. 307-322.

Kielhorn, F. 1888. Chamba copper-plate inscription of Somavarmadeva and Asatadeva, Indian Antiquary, Vol. XVII, January 1888, pp. 7-13.

Kielhorn, F. 1892a. Inscriptions from Khajuraho, Stone Inscription of Yasovarman of the year 1011, Epigraphia Indica, Vol. 1, 1892, pp. 122-135.

Kielhorn. F. 1892b. The Bhela-ghat Stone Inscription of Queen Alhanadevi, Epigraphia Indica, Vol. II, pp. 7-17.

Kielhorn. F. 1892c. Nagpur Stone Inscription of the Rulers of Malava, the (Vikram) year 1161. Epigraphia Indica, Vol. II, pp. 180-194.

Kielhorn, F. 1896-97. Khalimpur Plate of Dharmapaladeva, Epigraphia Indica, vol. IV, 1896-97, pp, 243-254.

Majumdar, R.C. 1933. The Kingdom of Kira, in The Indian Historical Quarterly, Vol. IX, No. 1, pp. 11-17.

McArthur, H. 1956. Central Lahul, Alpine Journal, 279-295.

Mirashi, V.V. 1937-1938. Rewah Stone Inscription of the time of Karna, the (Chedi) year 800, Epigraphia Indica, XXIV, pp. 101-115.

Nautiyal, Vinod, et. el. 2014. Lippa and Kanam: Himalayan Cist Burial Culture and Pyrotechnology in Kinnaur, Himachal Pradesh, India, in Antiquity, volume 88, issue 339. March 2014.

Sharma and Bhalla. 1987. Internet, 25.5.21.

Sircar, D.C. and A.N. Lahiri. 1959-60. No. 46, Footprint Slab Inscription from Nagarjunikonda, Epigraphia Indica, Vol. XXXIII, 1959-60, Archaeological Survey of India, New Delhi, pp. 247-250.

Tobdan. 1987. Two Eleventh Century Translators from Zanskar, Journal of the Asiatic Society, Bengal, Volume XXIX, No.1, 81-85.

Vogel, J.Ph. 1909. Ancient Monuments of Kangra, ruined in the Earthquake, Annual Report, Archaeological Survey of India, 1905-6, pp. 10-27.

Vogel, J. Ph. 1929-30. Prakrit Inscriptions from a Buddhist Site at Nagarjunakonda, First Apsidal Temple Inscription, in Epigraphia Indica, Vol. XX, pp. 7-8, 22-23.

**Books in Pali**

Jagdish, Bhikkhu J. Kashyap (Ed.).1959. Apadana, Part-I & II, Pali Publication Board, Govt. of Bihar.

Muller. E. (Ed.). 1893. Paramatthadipani (Dhammapala's Commentary on the Therigatha), Pali Text Ssociety, London.

Nathmal Tatiya. 1976. Theragatha Atthakatha, Pramatthdipani, Nav Nalanda Mahavihar, Nalanda, Vol. I & II. 1976 and 1977.

**Books in Sanskrit-Hindi and Pali-Hindi**

Abhimanyu, Shrimannalal. 1999. Amarkosh Bhasha Tika, Chaukhamba, Varanasi.

Asvaghosh. 1999. Budhacharita, Chowkhamba, Varanasi.

Shastri, Swamidwarikadas. 1996. Dipavansa. Baudh Aakar Granthamala, Varanasi.

**Books in Hindi**

Dabral, Shivprasad. 1995. Uttranchal-Himanchal ka Prachin Itihas, Virgatha, Dogadda, Garhwal.

Prabhat Sharma. 2016. Manmohak Devdhara Pangi, Aurous Jalandhar.

Ranpatiya, Amar Singh. 2001. Gaddi, (Bharmaur ki janjatiya lok sanskriti evam kalayen), Himachal Kala, Sanskriti, Bhasha Akademi, Shimla.

Rahul Sankrityayan. 1948. Kinnar Deshme, Kitab Mahal, Allahabad, 2nd edition, 1956.

Rahul Sankrityayan. 1953. Himalaya Parichaya (1), Garhwal, Illahabad Law Journal Press, Illahabad.

Rahul Sankrityayan. 1958. Kumaon, Shaanmandal, Varanasi.

**Journals in Hindi**

Tobdan. 1973. Lahul ke vibhin naam (Different names of Lahul), Himaprastha, Shimla, December, 1973.

**Books in Bhoti/Tibetan**

Gergan, Yoseb. 1976. Ladagsr Gyal-rabs Chimed gTer, (History of Ladakh), Sterling, New Delhi.

gNas-chhen Dril-bu-ri dang Gandhola'i gNas-yig don-gsal bzhugs-so. block print of Khangsar, 1905.

Tashi Rabgias. 1984. History of Ladakh Called The Mirror Which Illuminates All, published by C. Namgyal Tsewang Taru. Leh, Ladakh.

Rinchhen Zangpo. 1977. Collected Biographical material about Lo-chen Rin-chen-bzan-po and his subsequent reembodiments, from the dKyil monastery, Spiti.

rGya-mtsho 'Jam-mgon 'ju mi-pham. 1979. skad gnyis shan sbyar rab-gsal nor-bu'i me-long, reprinted 1979 by T.S. Tashigang, Leh, Ladakh.

rGyal-ba rGod-tshang-pa'i rnam-thar in Rare Tibetan Texts from Lahul, reprinted by Topden Tshering, Lahul, 1974.

rTa-mgrin. 1997. Grub-chhen au-rgyan-pa'i rnam-thar.

sTag-tshang Ras-pa. a'orgyan mkha' 'gro'i gling gi lam yig thar-lam bgrod pa'i them-skas bzhugs-so, (Hemis Gonpa, Ladakh) xylograph.

# Index


**A**

Agrawala, V.S. 71
Alexander Cunningham 106, 137, 140
Ali, S.M. 46, 52, 68
Apadana 21, 22, 23, 24, 26, 27, 31, 37, 42, 147
Archaeology of the High Himalaya 43

**B**

Bhagirathi river 36
Bhanodi: The Halting Station 123
Bird's Eye View of the Geography of the Himalaya 150-151
Buddhism in Kuluta 19
Buddhism in Lahul 19
Buddhist site at Nagarjunikonda 50, 74

**C**

Census of 2011 99
Central Lahul 13, 14, 16, 140
Chandrabhaga Valley 142
Charles Horne 20, 21, 147
Chatterji, S.K. 45, 66, 67, 68, 69, 70
Colin Rosser 55, 60
Courses of the two rivers 13
Csoma de Koros 107

**D**

Daniel Wright 76
Dhotaka river 36
Diwakar Nath Acharya 103, 138, 144
Dorje, C 121, 122, 140, 149

**E**

Emperor Asoka 22

**F**

Fitzgerald Lee 57
Francke, A.H. 60, 85, 90, 102, 103, 104, 106, 122, 135, 137, 140, 149

**G**

Gandhala monastery 15, 16, 20
Gar-zha in Tibetan Literature 136
Gazeteer of 1904 128
Gazetteer of 1897 13, 14
Gazetteer of Almora 73
Gazetteer of Garhwal 72
Gozangpa 20, 110, 111, 112, 113, 118, 148
Great Triangle 13, 14, 16
Guge Burial Gold Mask 43

**H**

Haṃsavatī city 36
Himachal Pradesh State Museum at Shimla 148
Hiuen Tsiang 9, 10, 17, 19, 22, 64, 88, 89, 90, 91, 96, 102, 103, 104, 105, 106, 137, 138, 144
Hiuen Tsiang's Mo-lo-so and Other Countries Lying beyond Kuluta 102-107

**I**

Indo-Aryan languages 61

Inscriptions from Middle India 94
-Bhela-ghat Stone Inscription 96
-Inscription from Khajuraho 95
-Khalimpur Plate of Dharmapaladeva 94
Nagpur Stone Inscription 96
-Rewah Stone Inscription 95

**J**

Jasoorgarh Gonpa 119

**K**

Kalhan, other victories recorded by 94
Kanashi: Its Relationship with Tibetan 61
Kanashi: The Language of Malana 55
Khadiravaniya Revata 36
Kinnara and Kimpurusha 46, 54
Kinnara King from the Purana 52
Kinnara King from the Rajatarangini 52
Kinnara Malana 55-65
-Himalayan Culture 55, 60, 61
Kinnaras and Asvamukhi 46
Kinnaras: Different Names 50-54
Kinnaras in Art 47
Kinnaras in History and Art 45-49
Kinnaras in other Pali Works 26
Kinnaras in Pali Literature 24-44
Kinnaras in the Jatakas 25
-Bhallatiya Jatak 25
-Chanda-Kinnara Játaka 25
-Chanda-Parvata Jataka 25
-Kandina Jataka 25
-Sama Jataka 25
-Sarabha-Miga Jataka 25
Kinnaras: The Living People 52
Kinnara Theras living on the banks of river Chandrabhaga 32, 38
Kinnauri language 56, 62
Kīra, Etymology 86
Kīragrāma (Baijnath), a Kīra Settlement 81
Kīras and Buddhism 90
Kīras in Himachal Pradesh in Modern Times 97
-Kīras in Bharmaur, Chamba 97
-Kīras in Mandi 98
Kīras in Kashmir 86, 89
Kīras in Kashmir, origin of 89
Kīras in Middle India 92
Kīras in Modern Times 96
Kīras in the History of Himachal Pradesh 79
Kīras of Kashmir 79-101
Kīras: The Kings of Kashmir 91
Kīras, Tibetan or Yarkandis 85
Kiratas in Buddhist Literature 74
Kiratas: Inhabitants of the Eastern Part of the Himalaya 66-78
Kiratas in Uttrakhand 72, 73
Kiratas of Nepal 67, 75, 76, 78
Kiratas: The Inhabitants of Eastern Part of the Himalaya 70
Kora or Rangtsa 15
Krītya and the Kīra 88
Krītya (Ki-li-to) 88, 89
Krītyas in Ancient Indian Tradition 90
Kṛtyakāh, the people called 87
Kukkuta and Kuluta 8

**L**

Lahul: A Historical Sketch 144-149
Lahul: Different Names 135-143
Lalitaditya Muktapida and His Campaigns 93
Law, B.C. 22, 23, 25, 32, 51, 52, 67, 68, 72, 91
Linguistic Paradox 60
Linguistic Survey of India 60, 61

## M

Mahakappina, a highly praised Thera in the Pali literature 1
Mahakappina Thera: One of the most eminent disciples of the Buddha 4
Mahakappina Thera: The King of Kuluta 1-23
Majjhima in Kukkuta 7
Malanis: The Practitioners of Himalayan Culture 60
Mattoo, P.K. 138
Mongol Race 73
Monier-Williams 18, 90
Muttra Museum 46

## N

Naga Karakota Dynasty 93
Nagarjunikonda 50, 51, 74

## P

Pangi: A Historical Review 127-134
Pangi Village Survey Report 1961 131
Paramatthadipani, Dhammapala's Commentary on Theragatha (Atthkatha) 26, 29
People's Geography of Lahul 140
Pilgrims 108, 109, 110, 118, 119

## R

Rahul Sankrityayan 24, 45, 46, 51, 61, 62, 137
Rana Lakshmana, history of 82, 84
Rhys David 6, 9, 10
Rinchen Zangpo: The Pathfinder 124
Rinchhen Zangpo 104, 105, 107, 115, 124, 125, 126, 145, 147, 148
River Chandrabhaga 1, 7, 11, 12, 13, 14, 17, 18, 19, 21, 22, 23, 24, 26, 27, 28, 29, 30, 31, 32, 37, 38, 40, 42, 43, 50, 125, 127, 135, 138, 145, 146, 147, 151
River Chandrabhaga, History of the 18
Rohtang Atal Tunnel 134, 149

## S

Shukla, L.K. 48, 72
Sindhu River 35
Singh, G.P. 70
Sircar, D.C. 46, 51, 109
sTag-tshang Raspa 109, 114, 115, 117, 118, 148
Sun temple of Martand 94
Sylvan Levi 76, 77

## T

Tashi Tamphel 148
Theragatha, an important ancient Pali work 1
Theragatha: Its Place in Pali Literature 22
Theragathapali 27
Therapadana 26, 31, 32, 42
Theras living on the Himalaya mountains 32
Theras living on the Lakes 34
Theras living on the River Chandrabhaga, not Kinnaras 31, 37
Theras living on the sides of rivers 35
Theri-apadana: Kinnari Theris living on the banks of river Chandrabhaga 40
Theriapadana: Kinnari Theris living on the banks of river Chandrabhaga 32
Tibetan connection of Kanashi 63
Tibetan Inscriptions from Bharmaur 122

Tibetan Pilgrims and the Monasteries in Chamba dedicated to Tibetan Buddhism 119
Tibetan Pilgrims Going to Jalandhara and Uddiyana 108-126
–Pilgrims' Route 109
Tinan valley 112, 141, 142, 143
Tribe, W.H. 56

**U**

Upadhyaya, B.S. 24, 46, 47, 53, 68, 69
Urgyanpa 20, 110, 112, 113, 114, 118, 148

**V**

Vinod Nautiyal 43
Vitasta (Jhelum) River 35

**W**

Wilson, H.H. 94, 138

**Y**

Yeshe Dorje 121, 122
Yeshe Rabphel Ritro 43

●●●

# Plates

Plate 1. Chhokhor, Drolma (Tara), 2015

Plate 2. Chhokhor, Bodhisattva, inscription on the back, 2015.

Plate 3. Chhokhor, Sharda, inscription, 2015.

Plate 4. Chhokhor, imprint of Sharda inscription, 2015.

Plate 5. Tinan, Rock carving, three Bodhisattvas, c. 2010.

Plate 6. Tinan, rock carving, detail of the middle figure, c. 1980.

Plate 7. Detail, Bodhisattva on right of viewer, Tinan rock Carving.

Plate 8. gZungs, Gundhla Khar, c. 1975.

Plate 9. Kora, gyamchhod, 2009.

Plate 10. Kora, stone cairns, 2009.

Plate 11. Kora, Stupas, 2009.

Plate 12. Gandhala, Drolma Chhudong.

Plate 13. Gandhala, Bodhisattva, marble, 1957.

Plate 14. Gandhala Vase

Plate 15. Srangbar, rock carving, 2010.

Plate 16. Srangbar, Rock Carving, front, 2010.

Plate 17. Srangbar, front, left of viewer, 2010.

Plate 18. Srangbarr, Rock Carving, backside, 2010.

Plate 19. Khangsar, Khangsar Castle, c. 1980.

Plate 20. Khyung, Chhukutsi gonpa, 2006.

Plate 21. Kolong, Child Buddha, 2010.

Plate 22. Karing, manye, 2010.

Plate 23. Karing, pillar base-i, 2010.

Plate 24. Karing, pillar base-ii, 2010.

Plate 25. Karing, mendicant Buddha, 2010.

Plate 26. Kardang, Three Bodhisattvas.

Plate 27. Kyelang Dusku, 2009.

Plate 28. Buddha Shakyamuni, Zholing.

Plate 29. Bodhisattva, Zholing.

Plate 30. Gushal, two unidentified stone sculptures, 2015.

Plate 31. Triloknath, parasol, 2016.

Plate 32. Inner room of Gepang's temple at Sissu, 2008.

Plate 33. Khangsar, women weeding, 2010.

Plate 34. Jamlung, Jambhala, Malana, photo Tej Ram Negi, 2012.

Plate 35. Malana, Jana'g, 2008.

Plate 36. Malana, Pirhe, photo.

Plate 37. Malana, Phagli, 2020.

Plate 38. Malana, Women dancing, Small Phagli.

Plate 39. Malana, body of Gepang being dressed, 2008.

Plate 40. Malana, Men in traditional dress, 2020.

Plate 41. Malana, Playing pa'z, 2020.

Plate 43. Guge image

Plate 44. Yaksha

Plate 45. Yakshee